D0830835

A SEASIDE
PRACTICE

A SEASIDE PRACTICE

Tales of a Scottish Country Doctor

Dr Tom Smith

With illustrations by Lesley Anderson

✳ SHORT BOOKS

First published in 2007 by
Short Books
3A Exmouth House, Pine Street
London EC1R OJH

10 9 8 7 6 5 4 3 2 1

A CIP catalogue record for this book
is available from the British Library.

Illustrations copyright ©
Lesley Anderson 2007

ISBN 978-1-904977-84-1

Printed in Great Britain by William Clowes Ltd, Beccles, Suffolk

Characters referred to in *A Seaside Practice* are composite characters, and essentially the author's inventions, although everything that takes place is based on real incidents.

For Mairi

Chapter One
First Appearances

I had arrived in Collintrae on April Fool's Day, 1965 – not an auspicious date. On April 8th, the local newspaper, the *Carrick Herald*, kindly featured me on the front page. 'NEW DOCTOR SETTLES IN' was the muted headline, and my career, from my birth in Glasgow to my schooling in Lincoln, and my medical training in Birmingham, was politely reviewed. I would have been encouraged were it not for the article immediately beside it.

Its headline was in larger, much bolder print. 'FIVE DEATHS IN THE STINCHAR COMMUNITY IN ONE WEEK. UNPRECEDENTED TRAGEDIES.' Under it were five photographs of recently deceased people, all of whom would appear to have shuffled off their mortal coil in direct reaction to my arrival in the area. Apparently, the paper's staff had looked up the records. Never before had five people from our little collection of villages died in one week. It didn't matter that I hadn't actually seen any of them. Four had died in hospital and one in a road accident miles away, but the connection seemed sure and augured ill. The local newspaper obviously felt the same. It seems that I was too young and, worse still, I had qualified in England.

With this less-than-encouraging coverage in the local press, I had to tackle my first day as doctor, and this was to take place in Braehill, one of the three villages under my care. The surgery there was in the house of a Mrs Jeanie Braidfoot, and had been fully kitted out by the previous doctors, all of whom had stayed a while then left for better, bigger and less solitary practices. Like a mother hen, Jeanie had looked after my predecessors, and the tradition would, it seemed, continue with me.

Seven or eight elderly ladies were busy chatting in Mrs Braidfoot's front room, which served as my waiting room. They didn't look ill. They could have been there for afternoon tea, not to see me. But see me they were determined to do. And it became clear that it was I, not they, who was to be examined and assessed. These ladies had seen off five doctors in the last decade, and they were going to add another one to their list.

My initial glance at the room had missed a much younger woman, who had been sitting behind the door. When I called for the first patient, she walked across the hall into the room that served as the surgery. My first thought was relief: she looked well and happy enough. I didn't have the sinking feeling that can come when an obviously ill person walks into the room. That is, until she rolled up her sleeve.

On the front of her forearm, just above the wrist, was a skin problem that I had never seen before in a person – only in gory photographic detail in my 'skins' text-books. It was a lump about two centimetres across, fiery and infected, raised above the skin and with a thickened edge. It looked horribly sore. Mary Bryant, its 'owner', said it wasn't. In fact, it was painless.

This wasn't good news. If it wasn't painful, all my training suggested that it was malignant. The medical name for it was a 'squamous cell cancer', and at that size it was surely very advanced. It had appeared and developed in only a week, so I assumed it was growing extremely fast. With a sense of real foreboding I reached for the telephone.

I was lucky. The consultant in 'skins' was doing a clinic in Ayr that afternoon, and if I could get Mary up to him before it closed, he would see her that day. But the conversation took a curious turn. It went something like this:

Me: I'm worried that this young lady has a very fast-growing lesion on her wrist. It looks like a squamous cell problem.
The dermatologist: Oh yes? And what does she do, this lady?
Me: She's a shepherd's wife.
The dermatologist: Oh yes? And how long have you been in Braehill?
Me: I started today.
The dermatologist: OK. Send her in. I'll see her for you.

Ayr was an hour's drive away, so I wrote a letter to the dermatologist, gave it to her and packed her off. I expected to hear later that she had been admitted to hospital.

At around four o'clock, the phone rang. I was still wading through my queue of elderly ladies. It was the dermatologist. The conversation was brief and to the point:

Him: So where did you train, Doctor?

Me: Birmingham.

Him: Not many sheep in Birmingham, then?

Me: Er, no.

Him: You've just sent me a case of orf.

Me: Pardon?

Him: Orf. Sheep pox. She's caught it from feeding a lamb. Never heard of the Folies Bergères?

Me: Pardon?

Him: The Shepherdess Follies. It's in Paris. Read up about it. Welcome to the district. And don't worry, you're not the first to make that mistake.

Me: So how do I treat it?

Him: You don't. It gets better on its own. Wait and see.

The dermatologist, Tommy Cochrane, and I eventually became great friends. We looked after many patients together, but he never let me forget that first conversation. Orf has three lines in the most complete textbook of medicine, and doesn't appear in any of the others. It's related to smallpox and cowpox. Only people who work with sheep catch it, and once infected they are immune for life from further 'orf' attacks and from other pox viruses. Lambs get it around their mouths, and it spreads to humans who have to bottle-feed them.

So why the reference to the Folies Bergères? It's simple. Sheep farmers and their shepherdesses would catch orf at an early age. All it produced was that one patch. Sheep pox doesn't spread further in humans. So when the mark had healed, they would remain unscarred and, crucially, immune from smallpox. Two hundred years ago, everyone else caught smallpox. The survivors were 'pock-marked' – with pitted scars all over their bodies, and particularly their faces. Only shepherdesses and milkmaids (who caught cowpox in the same way) had smooth features and healthy complexions. So the Folies recruited shepherdesses for their shows.

My episode with Mary Bryant didn't do me any harm. Mary was a newcomer to the village and to farming and didn't know about orf. If she had been a born-and-bred local she wouldn't have bothered me with such an obvious problem. But the locals understood that I had done my best for her, and that was all, I hoped, that mattered.

CHAPTER TWO
COLLINTRAE

The sleepy village of Collintrae lies on the south-west coast of Scotland, and stretches along a long single shoreline. Seen from the sea, there is a row of fisherman's cottages bordered to the west by a solid sandstone harbour wall. Behind these cottages, more protected from the winter storms, is the heart of the village, where the landsmen, farm workers and foresters live. Where the village road meanders eastwards up the River Stinchar's north bank towards the higher country, there's a smattering of bigger houses for teachers, bankers, lawyers and businessmen – the commuters to Girvan thirteen miles to the north. In its single main street stands Collintrae's one church, three pubs (the

Ayrshire Scot has his priorities right) and three shops.

Seven miles up river, along that meandering road, lies Kilminnel, the centre for the local dairy and arable farmers, cosily settled into the valley floor, alongside rich alluvial fields and looking across at low, green, rolling foothills. And eight miles further on is Braehill, higher still, nestling in the valley between steeper, browner, heather-clad hills, where the sheep and beef cattle, grazing there all year round, have been enough to keep families reasonably comfortable for hundreds of years.

It is these three villages of Collintrae, Kilminnel and Braehill that made up my practice, which stretched twenty miles along the coast road from north to south, and thirty miles eastwards from the shores of Collintrae – six hundred square miles in all. With just eighteen hundred human inhabitants, that's just three people per square mile. They were all my responsibility. There were also around a hundred thousand sheep and twenty thousand beef cattle. Thankfully they were the vet's domains – or so, in my initial innocence, I thought.

It had been my wife Mairi who had found the advert in the *British Medical Journal* for the vacancy in Collintrae. It was a long way from my last position in Birmingham – both in miles and in atmosphere. To be

16

frank, I had seen my future in the Midlands. The usual house jobs in a big busy hospital, followed by a first GP appointment in a large practice in the northern outskirts of the city, were typical career moves for a young doctor on the way up.

Three things got in the way of that ambition. One was my wife, Mairi, an island Scot. She was never going to settle so far from the sea. We once drove from Birmingham to Aberystwyth and back in a day, just so she could see it. What we actually saw was rain – all the way – and an absolute absence of parking spaces when we got there. We drove along Aberystwyth esplanade, stopped for a few seconds to buy an ice cream from a van, causing a traffic jam as we did so, and headed home. But Mairi had seen the sea once more and her mind was resolutely made up.

My senior partners, Dr Dai and Dr Owen, were the second block to my advancement in Birmingham. They had qualified in Wales at the beginning of the war, had joined the army together, served in North Africa together, and been captured together when they had volunteered to stay behind to tend the injured after the British had to retreat from Rommel. Their experience, they thought, had forged a lifetime friendship, so when the war was over, they decided to go into partnership.

They were so close that they would willingly share, without the proverbial paddle, a canoe up the Orinoco.

Sadly, by the time they decided to employ me, in 1964, their friendship had long been lost. They were paddling in opposite directions and the canoe had sunk without trace. No longer speaking to each other, it was their habit to communicate, and then only when absolutely necessary, by hand-written notes. Until I arrived, the note-carrier had been one of the receptionists, but the job, along with many others that I had never been trained for by my teachers in medical school, now fell to me.

They were short notes, usually referring to patients and their mistrust of each other's diagnoses, the part that I was permitted to know about being written in English. The rest was written in Welsh and was evidently even less polite. I never found out exactly why they were so hostile to each other, but I got the impression that it was something to do with their wives, and the way their incomes were split.

It all came to a head for Mairi and me one week, during my third month in the practice, when my first pay cheque was due. Mairi and I were wet behind the ears. I should have read the warning signs – the arguments between my partners and the huge extra load of

18

work that I was expected to do in comparison to them. Our verbal agreement had been that I would be given a small advance each month to tide me over until I received my share of the practice income after three months. My gross pay was to be £2,500 a year – a colossal sum in those days – paid in three-monthly instalments from then onwards.

So Mairi and I were looking forward to our £600 or so. We had a mortgage and a car loan to pay, and the overdraft had been growing apace since we had left the hospital residency. The cheque that arrived, however , was for £300, which would make my salary something nearer £1,400 a year. That evening I was in the branch surgery, which was attached to the senior partner's house. I got there early, to ask about the discrepancy. The senior partner, Dr Dai, wasn't there, but his formidable wife, Miriam, was. Miriam was the self-appointed practice manager and treasurer and, as the senior partner's wife, she was well aware of her dominance over a new junior GP.

She put me right. There were a few things to come off my salary, she said – didn't I know about them? Because Dai owned the buildings of both the main and branch surgeries, Owen and I had to pay him rent for using them. We also had to pay our share of their cleaner's and gardener's pay for keeping the practice premises neat and tidy. And there were all sorts of other practice expenses that had to be shared among the three of us. So the gross of £2,500 was quite legitimately whittled down to £1,400 – and that was before income tax. She reminded me that as the years progressed I would, step by step, earn a larger share of the profits, but I had to be patient. One day, she implied, I would be just as respected in the district as her saintly husband.

She then handed me the draft partnership agreement (which had taken her three months to draw up). Could I take it home this evening and study it? All parties could sign it later in the week.

I started that evening's surgery in a suppressed fury. I hope it didn't show on my face as I entered the waiting room to be greeted by around forty car body workers and tyre makers, all hoping to have their private sick notes signed. It was a Thursday evening. They had all signed off work sick on Monday morning: to get a full week's wages from the car or tyre plant they could miss Monday to Thursday, but they had to get back to work on Friday, so this was the evening for their back-to-work notes. If they were really ill and were off a whole week, they only got half pay. These patients certainly knew how to work the system.

I have no reason to suppose it was any different in any other industrial practice. In the English Midlands, the vast majority of work sickness absence stretched from Monday to Thursday. Friday was, apparently, a day of amazing good health. Manufacturing employers must have known that this was a tad odd, but had no answer to the power of the unions who had negotiated the rules – or indeed to the connivance of doctors like Dai and Owen, who were doing very well, thank you, from the sick note fees.

I struggled through that evening surgery, slowly simmering with the injustice of my pay and the waste of my time by people so obviously on the 'take'. My first patient had had 'backache' on Monday and had been signed off by Dai. It was better now, Doctor, he said. So could he have a note to go back to work tomorrow, please?

Anger must have clarified my mind. I decided to examine his back. No one had done that before. He protested: there was no need for that, his back was perfectly okay now. It must have just been a muscle strain, he suggested, helpfully. I insisted: I wouldn't be a good doctor, I said, if I didn't examine him properly. After all, I might miss a slipped disc or arthritis, or even kidney or prostate trouble. He lay down on the couch. I bent him and stretched him, pummelled him and prodded him.

It's easy to make a back feel sore, even when it's normal. A judicious prod here, a bit of pressure there, and you can make your patient yelp. Of course, it isn't ethical or moral, but it sure is satisfying. My patient yelped.

'Oh,' I told him, sounding suitably serious. 'Your back obviously isn't right yet. Especially as you have such a heavy job in the factory. You had better stay off until we can sort out the cause and get it completely better. I'll arrange for some X-rays. In the meantime I'll sign you off for another two weeks.'

He was thunderstruck. He knew, and he knew that I knew, that he was having me on. His back was as good as mine. He protested again that the pain was nothing. I prodded him again just on the spot where the sciatic nerve emerges from between the third and fourth lumbar vertebrae. He yelped again.

'There you are,' I said triumphantly. 'You still have pain. You can't go back to work yet. Here's your official sick note. You don't have to pay for it, so that'll save you paying us for a private one.' I tore a sheet from the NHS pad, rather than the thicker one for private notes, and started writing. Official sick notes from the NHS didn't cost a penny – they were used for longer spells off work, and were free.

'I don't want it,' he raged at me. 'I'll go back to work tomorrow anyway. And I'll see Dr Dai in the future.' He pushed himself off the couch with amazing agility and speed for someone so recently troubled by a bad back, and stomped out.

I wrote up his notes meticulously, suggesting that we should investigate the repeated back problems that had kept him off work so many times in the previous year, stacked them away on my out-tray, stood up and walked with a sigh to the door, to usher in the next patient.

I was surprised to see that half of the people in the waiting room were getting up to go. Patient number one had tipped off patients numbers two to twenty that I was 'an examining doctor' and didn't hand out work notes to order. I was no use to them and they had decamped, grumbling into the Birmingham night.

The evening surgery continued in a better mood, until close to its end. As I was talking to my last patient, a commotion from the waiting room interrupted us. I excused myself, and went to see what it was about. Lying on his back across three seats was a tramp, attended by two policemen. He was a stranger to me, which was unusual – by this time I had got to know most of our small colony of homeless and vagrants.

One of the officers apologised for bringing him in. They had found him slumped on a bench in a nearby park. They had thought he was drunk, but he was complaining about a stomach pain, and they felt they had better bring him to me before taking him in for a night in the cells, where they could at least give him food and warmth. The police, incidentally, have been like that wherever I have worked, in Birmingham or Ayrshire.

The man himself looked around fifty years old, though he could have been thirty. Homeless people, like prime ministers, age faster than the rest of us. They probably have similar levels of stress. He was filthy, hadn't washed or shaved for weeks, and had obviously starved for several days. His cheeks were sunken and flushed, he was breathing heavily and didn't smell, even faintly, of drink. He was pleased to see me, again an unusual reaction in a down-and-out.

One of the policemen helped me to undress him. He was in a lot of pain, and his stomach was as stiff as a board. As I felt his abdomen, he winced, and the muscles below my fingers tensed into a hard solid sheet. His pulse was fast and thready and his blood pressure low.

It took seconds for me to recognise that he had peritonitis, either from a ruptured appendix or from a perforated stomach ulcer. My only option was to get him straight to hospital from the surgery. There was a blanket on a chair near the couch, so I asked one of the officers to make him comfortable by wrapping it around him, while I reached for the phone. Within a quarter of an hour, he was on his way by ambulance. I thanked the policemen, and looked at the time. The surgery had taken from five-thirty until nine o'clock. I phoned home, to apologise for being so late, and left the surgery with the blanket folded on the couch.

Mairi was used to my late arrival in the evenings, and wasn't upset. I don't know how she did it, but there was always hot food ready whenever I arrived after surgery, along with a small whisky and water. There were times when I was so tired that all I wanted was the drink.

After supper, we sat together to study the practice agreement. It was full of the usual restrictions prevalent at the time. If I were to leave the practice, I could not practise within the surrounding fifteen miles. That was to stop me 'poaching' patients from them. It would take ten years for my pay to achieve 'parity' with that of the other partners, but the work would be equally shared amongst us. Except that the senior partner would take three fewer surgeries per week, to manage the finances and organise the practice and the buildings. The senior partner would not have to do evening surgeries more than once a week, and would have two weekends off per month. That was, apparently, because he was older and had spent many years building up the patient numbers, and deserved a little extra. The clauses about us paying part of the gardener's and cleaner's wages were included. It was interesting that, although I was to be paid a lot less than the others over these future ten years, I was expected to pay a full third of the practice expenses. So the proportion of my income taken off for all these expenses was much greater than for the other two partners.

The proposed agreement was so unfair that we began to laugh. Not in a million years were we going to stay. But the biggest laugh was in the final paragraph. It ran something like this:

If the sons of the senior partner and of any subsequent partners qualify in medicine and wish to join the practice, then the senior partner's son shall have seniority.

I had an extra whisky on the basis of that one. The next day, we decided, we would start looking for a practice in Scotland. Preferably one without partners and, of course, near the sea.

The third thing that sent me packing happened early the next morning, and made my mind up once and for all. Just before I set out for the morning surgery, a man came to the door carrying a large brown paper parcel. A label on it stated it was for 'Dr Smith's Wife'. Mairi was excited. The outside label didn't list the sender, but it was obviously a gift of some sort, perhaps from someone who knew that she was expecting our first baby. This was the first sign of thanks from anyone in the practice in the three months we had been there.

Just as pleased, I stayed behind for a few minutes to see what it was. It was the blanket the tramp had been wrapped in the evening before. Miriam had sent a note with it. There were no pleasantries. I remember the exact words today, forty years on. They were in capital letters, indicating the writer's anger:

YOUR HUSBAND HAS ALLOWED THIS
BLANKET TO BECOME INFESTED WITH
FLEAS AND I HAVE NO INTENTION OF
LAUNDERING IT MYSELF. WE NEED IT
CLEAN AND UNINFESTED FOR NEXT
MONDAY MORNING SURGERY.

There was not even a signature, or 'kind regards', although I suppose kind regards would have been hypocritical under the circumstances. Luckily Mairi has a sense of humour: she just laughed it off. I, by this stage, was beyond incandescent.

The blanket was laundered and delivered on time. I didn't ever have a conversation with Miriam again, nor did I sign the agreement. I still spoke to Dai, who was strangely subdued with me. I suspect he was deeply ashamed of his wife's behaviour, but neither of us broached the subject. He wasn't surprised when I didn't sign and return the proposed agreement.

He did, however, try to remonstrate with me about sick notes. Apparently, he had been wakened at seven-thirty that morning by about a dozen men wanting sick notes to go back to their morning shift that day. They couldn't wait until the surgery opened at nine, because by then the shift would have started, and they would have lost half their week's wages. They had accused me of 'not co-operating' and being an 'examining' doctor when all they wanted was their usual note. I looked at him, sitting comfortably in his big leather consulting armchair. In his mid-fifties, he had long since stopped wanting to rock the boat. The income from work notes was a good extra for the practice, from which he stressed I would assuredly receive my share. If I didn't toe the line with them, we would lose a lot of patients to the McKelvie practice down the road – after all, they were doing the same thing – so that wouldn't do, would it?

I wish I could write here that I stood on a matter of principle and argued the toss with him, but I didn't. Instead I came to a compromise.

'If you like,' I said, 'I'll do regular Friday evening surgeries instead of the Thursday ones. Then you can collect all the work note money and you won't need to share it with me – you and Owen can keep it all to yourselves.'

Amazingly, the insult implied in the last suggestion washed over him. He was delighted by both propositions and we stuck to them until I left. I didn't bother, either, arguing about the salary. I put it down to experience and accepted the loss.

I didn't take long to leave. Mairi found the advert and we applied for it. At the interview it turned out that there were two adjoining practices – Braehill and Collintrae – that were both currently without doctors. The Braehill doctor had left to join a city practice, and the Collintrae doctor had left for the great surgery in the sky. My interviewers asked me if I would consider combining them, and I responded with the enthusiasm of the young, keen and wholly inexperienced.

The other interviewees were clearly older and wiser doctors looking for an easier time, for I was given the job.

Chapter Three
Getting There

The Collintrae practice, with its location on the shores of the Firth of Clyde, had won Mairi over before we had even arrived. Our journey there, however, was enough to dampen even the brightest of spirits. Mairi had only just given birth to our first child, Catriona, when we left the practice in Birmingham. An uncle of mine had a friend with a haulage business whose lorries often travelled loaded from Scotland to the Midlands and empty back again, so he offered help with the move. We would only have to pay about a tenth of the usual removal rate – to cover the fuel for the extra hundred miles of detour the driver would have to make on his return to Glasgow – for which we were extremely grateful. What we didn't expect was a brick lorry to turn up at our door. Granted there were no bricks on it, but the dust was there, and there were no sides. Our precious few possessions were to be hauled on a flat-back and covered with a tarpaulin. It was up to us, too, to load it. The driver was on his own and naturally couldn't shift the furniture by himself.

Mairi, game as she was, was hardly in a fit state to help. She had had a long and exhausting labour and was breast feeding. With no parents around us to help with the baby (we were both the children of older parents, who lived hundreds of miles away), she had still to function as a doctor's wife, as I worked out my final few weeks of partnership. Drs Dai and Owen extracted the full working time from me – there was no thought of paternity leave then. So I had to do my last surgery, then come back early to help load the lorry.

Somehow the driver and I managed to heave our things aboard, spread the tarpaulin over them and tie it down. We gave the driver directions and then watched everything we owned vanish into the March fog, as Mairi, Catriona and I climbed aboard our Morris 1100 and set off for the north ourselves.

It sounds simple, doesn't it? A happy little family heading homewards. We planned to take the eight-hour journey to Ayr, where Mairi's mother lived, in easy stages. We would stay there overnight, then drive down to Collintrae to meet our lorry at the gates of our new home.

We didn't bargain for two complications. The first was nappies. Mairi had been told of these miraculous new watertight disposable nappies for travellers. We could change the baby at strategic points en route, and leave all smells behind us. Fat chance. Whoever had made the claims about those nappies was deceiving the public. Within minutes, we seemed to have, for the want of a better word, breast-fed baby poo all over the inside of the car. The smell developed nicely as we travelled along, so that the air around us became unbreathable. We had the choice of the windows open and freezing to death, or windows closed and suffocating.

On top of that I had a dose of the runs. In the practice over the previous few days we had seen dozens of cases of diarrhoea and vomiting. We used to call it 'gastric 'flu'. Today we would glorify the infection by calling it an outbreak of Norwalk virus, or norovirus. By any name it smells as sweet. I had picked precisely the day of the removal to start my dose of it.

So with aching gut, having to stop every few miles – at every second pub or café – to deal with both my problems and Catriona's, we made slow and fitful progress up the map of Britain. We passed all those towns starting with W – Wolverhampton, Walsall, Warrington, Wigan – watching the new motorway beside us grow out of what appeared to be industrial desolation. The roadworks every few miles, as 'heavy plant' crossed the old A6 to the embryonic M-way, held us up further.

I'll draw a veil over the rest of that day. It's enough to state that we arrived in Ayr a full five hours later than planned. I had left most of my body weight in various conveniences on the way. The only one of us who took the journey in her stride was baby Catriona, who fed, slept and defaecated happily throughout. Mairi's widowed mum Bessie, delighted to see us, ushered us into the dining room. She had prepared a feast for us. I excused myself and threw up, for the twentieth time that day.

It wasn't a good start. The next morning we drove the forty miles to Braehill. The previous doctor's house in Collintrae wasn't yet available to us – his widow still occupied it. The last doctor in Braehill had lodged in the village, having used the practice as a temporary stepping stone to a better and bigger practice, and the room he had rented wasn't suitable for us either. So the kindly sisters at the convent in Braehill had offered us a cottage of theirs for the time being. We had a map, and we were to meet our brick lorry outside the cottage at around ten. Bessie came along with us. She couldn't help much physically, as she was frail, but she offered much-needed moral support and another pair of hands to hold the baby.

Still dehydrated, nauseated and with an aching gut, I finally drove up to our new home. Well, almost. The nuns hadn't told us that there was a rustic bridge just in front of the cottage, with a large sign beside it: 'Not suitable for vehicles of 5 tons or over'. No way was our brick lorry able to cross over, and the driver had stopped just short of it, blocking the way. He looked at us as if we were crazy. He couldn't believe that we had moved from the sophisticated city to this hovel in the boondocks.

Luckily, we had new neighbours. From the door of the adjoining cottage lurched Archie McLaren. We found out in the days to come that Archie always lurched. It was a combination of his continual intake of raw whisky and his work as a gamekeeper: his feet had constantly to deal with walking on uneven ground in the total absence of sensible messages from his sozzled brain about where they actually were in space. But Archie's heart was in the right place. He brought his tractor out from the shed behind our two cottages, and in a few trips across the bridge he had unloaded the lorry and emptied the contents into our new home.

Mairi and her mother started to sort out our goods and chattels, while I drove to the surgery to meet the outgoing doctor. She would pass on to me the details of patients she had been seeing, and I could pass onto her a cheque for the month's locum fee that I owed her.

Single-handed rural doctors were at that time appointed by the local authority health committee. After an interview conducted by local councillors and the departing Braehill doctor, I had been offered the job to start on March 1st. My Birmingham partners, however, had kept me to a three-month notice period, which meant that the first day I could start was April 1st. A retired GP living in the area had volunteered to step in when the previous Braehill doctor had left, and run the two practices up until March 1st. But from then onwards I was held to be responsible for them. The retired man had other commitments, so I had to find a locum to take my place for that month.

Of course, being in Birmingham, I had no way of choosing my locum, so the local medical committee had found one for me. Hence this meeting with Dr Theresa Mary O'Hara at Braehill that morning. A fifty-ish, feisty and single Irish woman, Dr O'Hara hadn't taken up the previous doctor's widow's offer of a room at her house in Collintrae. Instead, she had taken a room at the convent with the same nuns, who had made available for us their cottage. The sisters were initially delighted, it seemed, to have had the doctor in residence for the month. She had worked from there, being on call from the convent, which the patients, Presbyterian to a man and woman, found curious.

Dr Theresa was keen to get going. Most accents from the southern counties of Ireland are like music to my ears. I enjoy the softness and the rhythm, and usually warm to them. It wasn't like that with Dr Theresa. She was a small, thin, bird-like woman, and her voice was sharp and harsh, the words coming like machine-gun bullets, clipped at the edges. She was constantly fidgeting and twitching, crossing and uncrossing her legs, which were discreetly hidden under a long black skirt. She wore black sandals over thick woollen stockings. Her upper body was hidden in a rough grey sweater adorned with a plain metal chain necklace from the centre of which hung a large crucifix. I wondered, vaguely, what she did with it when bending over a patient. Did she sling it over a shoulder, to get it out of the way? I thought of gynaecologists I knew who wore bow ties, so that they wouldn't get in the way, but put the thought out of my mind as sacrilegious.

She rattled through the histories of cases she had seen in the month. I couldn't follow her in detail. My gut was still aching, the nausea hadn't completely gone, and I was half-asleep from our marathon of the day before. So my mind started drifting. As her voice faded into the background, my eyes wandered, stopping at a narrow bandage over the middle third of her left index finger. She was repeatedly rubbing and plucking at it, as if it were bothering her. The finger above the bandage was swollen and inflamed, and the redness was stretching towards the back of her hand.

She paused to sip her tea. I took the chance to ask about her finger.

'Have you hurt your finger?' I asked.

She looked down at it, then back at me. 'It's nothing. I cut myself opening a boil. It is a little infected, but it is healing now.'

It didn't look as if it were healing to me. I asked if she had taken an antibiotic for it, and whether she would like me to take a swab and send it to the lab.

'You never know,' I said, 'you may have a fairly virulent bacterium there. There are plenty of antibiotics here, so you could start on one now and I could send you the lab results later. Let me have your forwarding address, and we'll keep in touch.'

Dr Theresa drew herself up in her seat, stiff, erect and face flushed with anger. Although around ten inches shorter than me, she somehow towered over me.

'Young man,' she said, 'you are thirty years my junior. I won't take advice on how to treat a simple cut from you. And I'm certainly not taking an antibiotic. This will heal in its own time. Now if you don't mind, I'll take my cheque and leave. You will not be needing a forwarding address.'

'At least let me know whose boil you lanced, so I can check that that has healed, too,' I replied. I wasn't going to let her browbeat me, and there was something about that finger that disturbed me.

'If you must know, it was a man called Peter Morgan, an elderly gentleman in Collintrae. You'll find his address in the notes. Now if you don't mind...' Her voice drifted away. She took the cheque from me, rubbed her finger again, and walked out of my life and the lives of the people she had tended for the past four weeks.

Jeanie Braidfoot bustled into the room. On a small silver tray was a bottle of whisky, a crystal glass, and a piece of shortbread on a china plate. 'Welcome to

Braehill, Doctor. I'm thinking you will be needing this,' she said, smiling. It was only noon, but I took her advice, poured out a small dram, and sipped it.

That day I learned a lot about Dr Theresa and her month in the practice. She had already done the morning surgery, and my plan was to spend my first afternoon in the job going through the current problems in the practice. They weren't hard to find.

Dr Theresa had spent most of her time in the convent, virtually in retreat. She had made it plain to the patients that there were times when she should not be disturbed. She had hinted that she was preparing for a 'better life' and that they should all do the same. Physical health was not everything: they should be worrying instead about their immortal souls.

It wasn't a real surprise, therefore, that when families had needed her most it had been her rosary that she had brought out of her bag, rather than a stethoscope. I suppose in some countries that would have been appropriate. In South Ayrshire, where every village had Protestant martyrs' graves from the days of the religious wars, and where the Church of Scotland ruled, a rosary isn't the most effective or most acceptable of instruments with which to save a life. Its very appearance in the sick room was calculated to raise the temperature and blood pressure of patients and carers alike.

Just as bad was her attitude to birth control. She apparently agreed with G. K. Chesterton that it was 'no birth and no control'. Forthright in refusing the pill or any other form of contraceptive advice to the young women of the practice, she told them it was against God's law, and she wasn't having any of it. The pharmacy in Girvan, fourteen miles away, had been doing a roaring trade in Durex in the month in which she had held sway.

Faced with a groundswell of threats that the patients would leave the surgery and sign up with the Girvan doctors, Jeanie Braidfoot had done her best to hold the fort for me. 'This new young doctor winna be anything like Dr O'Hara,' she told them, hoping she was right. 'He'll soon get us all back on the richt road.' She must have been persuasive. There were no defections to Girvan so far.

Fortunately, on this my first day, there were no urgent calls, and I still had to see the Collintrae end, fourteen miles away, and visit the doctor's widow there. I thought I would take in a visit to Mr Morgan on the way. I looked through his notes, and saw that he had been retired in the village for around ten years. Before that he had travelled abroad a lot, first in the army, then as a diplomat in various Far East and European countries.

He lived in a cottage, one of around a dozen stretching along the shore road to the south of the village. I found out later that the polite locals called it Pensioners' Row: the others called it Death Row, as the only way people left these houses was 'feet first'. I very quickly learned a lot about local customs in those first few days. For example, the doctor always had to go out by the door he came in. It was very bad luck if he didn't. I never found out if the bad luck extended to the doctor, or was confined to the family inside. And, if people had to leave their house on a stretcher, they had to go head first never feet first, or they would not return. Feet first was only for coffins.

The cottages on the shore road had solid storm doors, behind which were less substantial front doors with frosted glass panels. Mr Morgan's storm door was open, so I rang the bell and waited on the step. After a moment or two, I could see movement through the 'frost'. Even through the glass I could see that the walk was slow and deliberate – a shuffle of short steps, as if very unsure of its foothold.

When the door opened, a thin old man faced me with

a puzzled look on his face. Immediately I felt that there was something wrong with his gaze, but couldn't quite place what it was. He was a classic 'elderly shabby', wearing what once had been high-quality clothes – a frayed suit, white shirt with a collar that had seen better days, tie not quite as neat as it should be, with a few food stains down it and the waistcoat.

'What can I do for you?' he asked, peering at me with those odd eyes, unfettered with glasses, even though he was in his late seventies.

'I'm Dr Smith, your new doctor. I thought I'd call round to check on your boil. I hear that Dr O'Hara lanced it the other day.'

'Boil?' he replied, as if it were new to him. 'I don't know about that. My memory's not what it used to be. Maybe Mrs Mitchell can help. She looks after me. She's through the back. Come in.'

He turned, and as he did so, he almost stumbled. He had to hold onto the wall for a second, to regain his balance. Then he shuffled with those short steps along the passageway into the kitchen, where his housekeeper was washing his dishes.

It began to dawn on me what might be wrong. The odd eyes, the walk, the memory loss, the boil, they were adding up to something I really didn't want to consider.

By the time he had got to the kitchen, he had already forgotten who I was and what I had come for. But he didn't seem to care. He sat down as if I weren't behind him, and stared vacantly out of the window.

Mrs Mitchell had heard the conversation at the door, and told me not to mind him. He was always forgetting things, but he was harmless. Yes, she had called in Dr O'Hara, because she had seen this boil on his back when she was helping to bathe him the other day. No, it hadn't been painful, but it did look very nasty, and Dr O'Hara had taken a lot of pus from it. Yes, she had noticed that Dr O'Hara had cut herself while doing it, but she hadn't bothered much – she had just wrapped a bandage around her finger, and gone off.

With much foreboding I asked Mrs Mitchell to help show me the boil. Mr Morgan was quite happy for us to manhandle him into position so that we could see his back in the daylight streaming in through the kitchen window. I was becoming less happy by the minute. Between his shoulder blades he had an ulcer – an open sore – with a raised edge all round it. I asked Mrs Mitchell what it had looked like before Dr O'Hara had opened it.

'It was just a raised lump,' she said. 'It didn't look like this. He never complained about it, like he would if it had been a normal boil. I don't think he even knew it was there.'

Mr Morgan's problems were all coming together into one diagnosis. We put his shirt back in place, and I walked around in front of him and sat opposite him, across the small kitchen table. I looked again into his eyes and recognised why I had found his gaze so odd. His pupils were different sizes, and they weren't exactly round. The best way to describe them was frayed at the edges, just like his clothes. I shaded them from the light with my hand, then took it away. There was no reaction: they were fixed in that position. They didn't enlarge with the light or diminish in the shade.

I was looking at eyes that had been described by a Dr Argyll-Robertson in Victorian times. He had been a specialist in syphilis. The shuffle, the balance problems, the memory loss, and most of all the 'boil' – in reality a swelling called a 'gumma' – all confirmed the diagnosis of the final stage of the disease. I had to get things moving, and fast, not just to get Mr Morgan treatment, but to let Dr O'Hara know what she had infected herself with.

My first task was to find Mr Morgan's next of kin. I had to tell whoever was the nearest relative what I had to do. Mrs Mitchell gave me the name of his son. My day suddenly went from very bad to even worse. For it turned out to be a name I knew very well, along with most doctors of my age. He was the Professor of Medicine at a British School of Medicine.

Suffice it to say that I dialled the Professor's number and, as expected, got his secretary. She sounded nice and efficient, and very protective of her boss. I asked to speak to the great man himself.

'I'm sorry, he is at a lunchtime discussion group at the moment,' she said. 'I'd rather not disturb him unless it's an emergency. Can I help? I do have the professor's confidence.'

I'll bet you have, I thought, but not for the news I'm about to give him.

'It's actually about his father,' I said, as coolly as I could. 'I'm his GP. I think the Professor would want to know about him as soon as possible. It is on the urgent side, and I ought to give him the news myself.'

'Oh dear,' she said, sensing that this was a bit out of the ordinary. 'Then I'll get him to the phone.'

I hung on. The phone was in the hall and I had carefully shut the kitchen door, to be out of earshot of Mrs Mitchell and Mr Morgan. To be frank, I didn't think Mr Morgan was still sensible enough to grasp anything I said, but I couldn't risk Mrs Mitchell hearing.

After a few minutes, the Professor's voice boomed in my ear. Did I know he was busy? Couldn't his secretary deal with it? He had been brought out of a very important meeting for this call. It had better be worth it.

'Well,' I started, 'your father is quite ill, and I think he needs admission.'

'Then send him up to my unit. I'll take care of him myself,' was the gruff reply. 'Send a letter with him, and I'll take it from there. You can give my secretary your particulars and phone number and I'll get in touch after I've seen him.'

Unbelievably, he was going to pass the phone back to his secretary. I had to get in fast.

'I think you had better hear the diagnosis first,' I muttered. As a student I had always felt intimidated by professors, and this was intimidation in spades.

'Why, what do you think he has?' came the voice again, a decibel or two above my comfort level. I wondered if the good Professor was deaf as well as domineering. I even started to muse on whether he had been born after his father had contracted his illness. Deafness is, after all, one of the signs of inherited... I put that thought to the back of my mind.

'Tertiary syphilis,' I said.

'What?' he bellowed. This time the decibel count was

far above earache level. 'Are you sure?'

'He has a gumma, dementia and Argyll-Robertson pupils,' I said, hoping that this was enough to convince him.

'Let me phone you back before you do anything further. I need to talk to someone.' This time the voice was more subdued. There was a click, then the burr of a vacant telephone line. I pondered on what to do next. I needed to find out where Dr O'Hara had gone. I took the chance that someone in the Health Board, who had employed her, might know.

I drew a blank. Dr O'Hara had left without telling anyone where she had gone, and was no longer available for locum duty. As soon as I put the phone down, it rang. It was the Professor again.

'Please send him into ward nine in Kilmarnock. Dr Gourlay will look after him there. Oh, and thanks for calling me.'

Kilmarnock is in North Ayrshire, around fifty miles from Collintrae. It wasn't too far away, but it was a long way from Professor Morgan's sphere of influence. I wondered if that was the idea. The boom in the voice had gone: it was still gruff, but low key. I sensed that his thanks were as close to an apology as he could get. He must be worried now about himself, I thought. I wondered how he would organise a syphilis test for himself – just in case he had it, too – and then turned to more important matters.

How could I contact Dr O'Hara? Obviously through the convent. I phoned the nuns to say that I would be on my way to see them. Mother Superior answered and asked if I could wait until after evening service at around seven o'clock. I was happy to agree. After seeing the still happy but confused Mr Morgan off in the ambulance to Kilmarnock, I drove into Collintrae village to meet the late doctor's widow. I was to start surgeries in her house the next morning, and we spent a few minutes sorting out details over a cup of tea, before I went home to see how the three ladies – Bessie, Mairi and Catriona – were getting on.

Apart from unpacking all the pots and pans, sorting out the crockery that hadn't been broken on the journey, cleaning all the brick dust from the furniture, unblocking a chimney, fixing a leak from the kitchen sink, preparing a meal, putting down the odd carpet, finding firewood for the fire, and getting rid of several dead mice, they had obviously had an easy few hours. Oddly, I didn't get any sympathy from them about my tortuous day. And when I said that I was going to visit the nuns at seven o'clock, they didn't seem too pleased.

The convent was just a hundred yards from the cottage, so I walked there. There was a half-moon, so I could see fairly well as I ambled along the path, thinking how different the work here was from the hustle in Birmingham. I was a little apprehensive, because I hadn't had any dealings with nuns before, but I needn't have worried.

The convent, before its current usage, had been an elegant country house, owned by a family that had done well in the Victorian heyday of industrial Scotland. The First World War had seen off their hopes for the future, and the Second World War had seen it turned into a hospital. There was no family left by 1945, so the church took the opportunity to buy the main buildings as a convent school. There were around ninety pupils aged from five to twelve, and thirty nuns. Around them was a large country estate that was now managed by the owner of 'the big hoose', the only other mansion house near the village. The nuns had no interest in the estate, so had let it out to their neighbour. That's why lurching Archie lived next door to us: he looked after the estate for the nuns and the big hoose and lived rent-free in the nuns' other cottage.

This much I had gleaned before I made this first visit. Armed with good vibes from Jeanie Braidfoot, who despite her staunch Protestant background said I would love the nuns, I strode up to the large wooden door, lifted the huge brass knocker and let it drop with a resounding clang. It opened slowly, and a tiny female figure, no more than four feet six inches tall, dressed in a full-length black habit, peered up at me. She had beer-bottle-bottomed glasses on, so I guessed she was virtually blind.

'You'll be the new doctor,' she said, with a beaming smile. 'You're very welcome, do come in. Just follow me, and I'll take you to Mother Superior.'

All I could see ahead of me was a wall of blackness, but I gathered that there was a corridor along which I had to stride after her. Naturally she knew every inch of that corridor and, with her poor eyesight, probably didn't realise quite how dark it was for someone coming out of the moonlit front court.

That's why halfway along the corridor I fell over something, only to land flat on my face on the wooden floor. My first impression was that I had tripped over a large upholstered stool, but it gave a yelp of pain and moved under my prone body. It took me a second or two to realise that it was the tiny nun. Once over the shock, she started laughing.

'I'm sorry, Doctor, we have a wee grotto here in the

wall with a wee statue of Mary Mother of Jesus in it. We kneel to it every time we pass, which is why you fell over me. That's a good start, assaulting the first nun you come across, isn't it?'

She went into peals of laughter again, and this time fetched a match out of a small purse, lit a taper from beside the statue of Mary, and showed me the rest of the way.

Mother Gabriel, the Superior, met me at the door with a cup of tea, then settled me into a comfortable chair in her room, before welcoming me to the district. She was a charming, educated, very good-looking woman of around fifty, with laughter lines around her eyes and a great sense of humour.

I asked if she knew anything about Dr O'Hara and where she had gone.

'A religious maniac that one,' she said. 'Spent far too much time on her devotions and not enough time having fun. She's gone to be a nun in Ireland, and I don't know what the others will make of her. We like a bit of a laugh here. I'll see if I can find the convent number for you, but I'd be surprised if she'll want to speak to you.'

She opened a small black book on her desk, dialled a number on her phone, then handed it to me, and left the

'My first impression was that I had tripped over a large
upholstered stool, but it gave a yelp of pain and moved
under my prone body. It took me a second or two to
realise that it was the tiny nun.'

room. I looked around while I was waiting for the answer. There was a wall full of books of all kinds, very few of them religious, many of them scientific – there was even Charles Darwin's *Origin of Species*. There were daffodils and crocuses nicely arranged in a small vase, and on the walls were rows of paintings obviously done by the pupils at the school, interspersed with photographs of past pupils and nuns. I liked what I saw, and knew I was going to get on well with them.

A voice from the phone brought me back to earth. It was the Mother Superior of the other convent. I explained that I was the doctor to the convent in Braehill, and had been given the phone number by Mother Gabriel. The voice at the other end softened. Could I give Mother Gabriel her very kindest best wishes? I promised certainly to do that. And then I asked if I could speak to Dr O'Hara.

I was told that it wouldn't be possible. Dr O'Hara had left the outside world and was in retreat. She had left instructions that she could not now communicate with people from her former life. I explained that I thought that she might be ill with a serious infection, and need treatment. I asked if she would please ask Dr O'Hara to come to the phone. I was told to wait for a few minutes, and then she returned with the message that the infection was healing perfectly well by itself, and Dr O'Hara felt there was nothing more to say. She certainly didn't want to speak to me about it. After all, I was far less experienced in these things than she was. The phone was put down, and that was the end of the conversation.

What more could I do? Of course the sore was healing. Primary syphilitic sores always do. But the disease doesn't vanish. It spreads, and in someone who had received such a big initial dose, it could lead to a fatal infection in months. If she would only take a short course of penicillin she would be fine.

Mother Gabriel returned. She could see I was troubled, but it was impossible for me, of course, to tell her why. She smiled, and reassured me that everything was for the best. God would look after Dr O'Hara in His own way.

I don't know whether or not He did, but around six months later, I noted a name in the *British Medical Journal*'s obituary page. Dr Theresa Mary O'Hara had died suddenly from an overwhelming infection in a convent in Ireland. There were no living relatives. I was sad that she hadn't heeded me. I was visiting the convent the day that the news broke. Mother Gabriel asked me if this had been what I had tried to warn her about. I said that it was. 'It was up to her, not you,' she said. 'But she was listening to a different call. Don't let it bother you.'

So I didn't.

CHAPTER FOUR
BREAKING ME IN

My baptism of fire in the practice continued the next morning. The phone rang beside the bed at around seven-thirty. A man's voice on the other end of the phone, agitated and breathless: 'Doctor, you'll hae to come quick. Maggie's drappit her mammy in the Muck.'

It was never thus in Birmingham. I stirred myself and uttered the word for which I would become famous over the next few weeks.

'Pardon?'

'It's mad Maggie. She's chucked her mither in the River Muck. The old lady's sittin' there, up to her waist, wi' a' her kitchen roon aboot her. Maggie's raging up and doon, yelling at her. It's at the cottage just below Muck Bridge.'

I threw on my clothes and looked at the Ordnance Survey map pinned to the wall. The River Muck (properly spelt Muick, from the old Scots, but the silent 'i' had long been forgotten) was a tributary of the Stinchar. Muck Bridge was on a side road between Braehill and Kilminnel, up in the hills, about six miles away. That wall map was essential to me in those first years. A previous doctor had printed, with meticulous neatness, the names of each family beside the names of each farm and croft. The Muck Bridge cottage bore the name McRobert, so I assumed that the old lady was a McRobert. Maggie I knew nothing of, but the phone conversation suggested that she wasn't too kindly disposed to her mum. The fact that the anonymous neighbour who had phoned had called her, without any malice, 'mad', suggested that she already had a reputation for erratic behaviour.

It took me ten minutes to get to the scene. There was Maggie, a tall, slender woman, ashen pale with anger, striding up and down the path beside the stream, throwing whatever was left of the kitchen into it. Sitting in the middle was a small, frail, elderly woman, her tear-stained face a slate-blue colour with the cold. Beside her

'It's Mad Maggie. She's chucked her mither in the
River Muck. The old lady's sittin' there... wi' a' her
kitchen roon aboot her.'

were two kitchen chairs, a table, a metal bin, and a washboard. Downstream from her, caught up round the stones in the bed of the stream were towels, aprons, tablecloths and even curtains that had been torn down and thrown in by the poor benighted Maggie.

The younger woman looked up at my car approaching and saw the police car only a few yards behind it. She flung her last items, an ironing board complete with iron, at her mother, turned and hightailed it up the hill behind the cottage, through the small grove of hazel trees and on to the moorland beyond. In minutes she had disappeared into the mist.

I wasn't immediately concerned about Maggie: she could wait. Her mother couldn't. The policeman and I waded into the water, which was about knee high, and gently carried the old lady into the house. It was wrecked. The stone and earth floor was covered with smashed dishes, cooking pots and old earthenware jars, from some of which a dark, sweet-smelling liquid had spilled. Cinders from the stove had been raked out and thrown around. Some were still glowing. We could see that we had to get the old lady dry, warm and out of there as soon as possible. We didn't know what that liquid was, but it smelled as if it could be flammable.

Neighbours soon rallied round, and one was glad

to take Mrs McRobert in for a few days while others agreed to put the place to rights. They would make sure the old lady was looked after. But what about Maggie?

Maggie was in her late thirties, and had been a nurse in a Glasgow teaching hospital until she had had to give up her career to look after her ailing mum, who had become frail and, to be honest, a bit 'odd', in the last few years. The alternative to Maggie coming home was for her to go into care, and Maggie hadn't wanted that. So the career had been put on hold for a while. There were rumours, of course, that this wasn't the only reason for Maggie's return home. Neighbours hinted at an affair that had finished and at Maggie wanting a fresh start.

The 'madness' had been a recent development. People had noticed that Maggie had become a bit irascible lately. She would get angry for no reason when she met old friends at the shop, and was no longer the outward-going, friendly young woman that she had been. She had stopped caring about how she looked: her clothes were dirty and unkempt. She smelled, and she now frightened the local schoolchildren. People put her change of character down to her lost love, or her approaching change of life (naturally a favourite scapegoat for many women's ills), while she and her mother had gradually become virtual recluses, dependent on one another, getting quietly crazier together, and withdrawing from all contact with friends and neighbours. No one had known that Maggie had been abusing her mother, however, until the episode at the bridge.

This was an odd story. While the police, assorted neighbours and volunteers started to roam over the hills above the cottage, searching for her, I returned to the Braehill surgery to find Maggie's notes. To my surprise the folder was thin, almost empty of any encounter between Maggie and the previous doctors. She had never shown a sign of mental illness in the past – which was completely at odds with her behaviour today. I had expected a 'thick note' syndrome. Look at any shelf of patients' notes in a doctor's surgery and you can instantly tell those who have long-term physical or mental illness. Their folders are far thicker than those around them – regular attendees often need two or three folders taped or banded together to hold all their records.

Two days later, Maggie was found still alive by the bank of a stream around six miles into the hills. She was cold and wet, but only semi-conscious. I admitted her to the psychiatric unit in Ayr and she began to recover, physically if not mentally. The consultant psychiatrist, Dr Whitelees, phoned me a few days later. He, too, was puzzled by Maggie's illness. She was still heavily sedated, so Dr Whitelees hadn't yet been able to pin down the cause, but he had found that she was very anaemic. He was asking a physician to see her.

Funnily enough I had asked the same physician to see her mother. She was anaemic, too, and didn't know who or where she was. She seemed to be living in her childhood and was constantly talking about going home to her long-dead parents. She had to be restrained from walking out of the house up to the ruin where she had lived as a schoolgirl. How could two women in the same house, with no previous history of mental problems, now be behaving so bizarrely? I'd heard of *folie à deux*, but this was ridiculous.

Their blood test results gave us the clue. An alert lab technician spotted that their red cells were mis-shapen and pale, and that there were too many basophils, a particular type of white blood cell, in their blood films. The basophils didn't look right – they had 'blobs' inside them that wouldn't be there normally. The technical name for the appearance was punctate basophilia and it meant only one thing.

I turned my mind back to the scene at the bridge. Mrs McRobert wasn't slate blue with cold and Maggie wasn't pale with anger. They were both grey with lead poisoning. That blood picture, their mad behaviour, and their appearance all fitted with only this diagnosis. We were told the blood biochemistry results minutes later. Maggie's blood lead level was a record for the lab. Surely her mother's would be the same.

I asked the local water board official to meet me at the cottage. The likeliest cause was contaminated water. One of the neighbours was in the living room when we arrived, cleaning up the mess and putting what wasn't broken tidily back on shelves and in cupboards. She had also put sand down on the floor to mop up the dark liquid. It was, she said, Mrs McRobert's famous bottled fruit and her best guess was that it came from blackberries. Like many people of her age the old lady spent each autumn gathering the fruits of the hedgerows and bottling them. Once the fruit had cooled, she poured the finished product into her glazed earthenware jars, family heirlooms that had come down to her over the years, and sealed them. Bottled fruits, she averred, tasted a lot better when they had been in one of her jars for a while.

All her neighbours got a present of her fruit every Christmas: they found that just one jar of the bitter-sweet contents was enough. Mrs McRobert, however, swore by their health-giving powers, and ate it regularly throughout the winter. Presumably Maggie did the same. We took a sample for analysis.

The next step was to test her water supply. We tried to turn on the kitchen tap. It sputtered a few drops of water, then stopped. The neighbour helpfully interrupted.

'Oh you won't get much out of that tap. They've had problems with the mains pressure since the frost two years ago. It's cracked somewhere and it hasn't been fixed yet. We're so far away from the town, you know. Luckily, the McRoberts have the old water tank supply. It's out there on the hillside.'

We walked up the hill about fifty yards to where the tank stood, covered with moss, above the house. A pipe led from it to a storage tank in the roof space, and the pipes from that led to the bathroom sink and the sink in the scullery. Only the cold water tap in the kitchen was connected to the mains, and that, it seemed, hadn't been used for a couple of years.

You have already guessed it. The tank on the hill, the pipes joining it to the tank in the roof, and the pipes to the other taps were all made of lead.

We worked it out over the next few days. The two women hadn't just been drinking lead-filled water; the earthenware glaze lining the pots was also stuffed with lead, and putting fruit inside them was the perfect way to leach it out. The two women couldn't have conceived a more efficient combination of circumstances by which to poison themselves.

Happily, lead poisoning is easy to treat. They were admitted, side by side, into a medical ward in the local hospital, and given drugs to draw the lead from their bodies. Within hours they felt better. Within days they were back home, the mains supply restored, and with strict instructions on how best to bottle fruit. The old lady consented to go into a care home, and Maggie went back to work. The 'mad' Maggie had gone for ever.

Chapter Five
Learning the Language and the Ropes

'Drapping mammy in the Muck' was just the beginning. Over the next few weeks I learned a new language, the Scots language that Burns had spoken two hundred years before, and that had hardly changed since he had died. It wasn't completely foreign to me. Although brought up in England, I was born a Scot and familiar enough with the Glasgow dialect of my uncles, aunts and cousins. As the calls came in over the next few days I got quickly up to speed. A few were fairly easy to translate.

A message that 'The wean's come oot in a wheen o' wee plukes' was quickly translated into 'The toddler (the wean) has suddenly developed (come oot in) a very large number of (a wheen o') small septic spots (wee plukes)'. In other words the child has chickenpox. 'Rabbie has been boakin'a'nicht' meant that 'little Robert has been sick all night'. For 'I'm fair scunnert wi' ma man' read 'I am heartily sick of my male partner'. 'Wee Eck has a croachle in his thrapple' translated into 'little Alexander has a rattling noise in his throat'. In fact that was an urgent one, as it suggested that he had croup, and might well choke, so wee Eck was dispatched post haste to the children's hospital in Ayr.

It seemed that time had stood still, too, in the Collintrae surgery. Dr Rose, my predecessor, had set up in the village in 1933, and had been happy to let the advantages of modern medicines pass him by. Taking my first surgery at his house had been a shock. It was so different from the well-maintained room in Braehill that had been adapted for the purpose by the previous two or three doctors. In Collintrae, a lean-to greenhouse against the side wall of the house doubled as the waiting room. A wooden bench served as the only seats for the patients: at most, five or six people could wait there at a time. An opening through the house wall led to a small hall, and then the consulting room. The door between the hall and room was thin: everything said above a whisper in the room could be clearly heard in the greenhouse-cum-waiting room. Dr Rose was not one, apparently, for confidential chats.

Against one wall of the consulting room was a Victorian chaise longue, that had, apparently, served as the examination couch, under which were several tatty cardboard boxes crammed full of files of notes. At the foot of the chaise longue stood three large Winchester bottles. They looked quite impressive: one was full of a milky white liquid, one was green and the third was brown. On a small table at the head of the chaise longue was a tray in which was a bottle with a glass stopper, beside which was a wire frame with a handle and a pile of muslin swabs. They were all dusty, as if they hadn't been used for a while – at least since Dr Rose had died. On the other side of the narrow room was a kneehole desk, at which was a comfortable, though well-worn, leather chair, and beside the end of the desk was a wooden chair with a plastic seat that had seen decidedly better days. One was obviously for the comfort of the doctor, the other for the discomfort of the patient. Chairs like this didn't encourage long conversations.

On the desk was a copy of the *British National Formulary* for 1933. It was well thumbed and very grubby. Many of the pages were dog-eared to make opening them at those pages easier. Several of the prescriptions on them were outlined in red ink, suggesting that they were the late doctor's favourite remedies.

I looked more closely at the three bottles. The white one was labelled 'stomach mixture', the green one 'tonic' and the brown one 'aperient'. I knew the purpose of the bottle with the glass stopper, the wire frame and the swabs, but only from memories of a visit I had made as a small boy with an uncle to the Wellcome Museum of Medicine in Gower Street in London many years before. I opened the stopper and took a very tentative sniff at its contents. It was chloroform: the mask and muslin were used to cover the patient's nose and mouth while the chloroform was dropped upon it. I could not think why it was in the room, and still apparently used. Chloroform had been abandoned as an anaesthetic in practice long before I had become a medical student: our generation was taught that it had been a good anaesthetic for its time, but that its propensity for causing acute fatal liver failure had toned down its popularity a tad.

The faint aroma of chloroform lingered in the room, so I opened the only window, took a deep breath of the cold April air, and asked my first patient to come in. A pale, frail, thin woman heavily clad in thick winter clothes shuffled in. She looked tired, in fact half-asleep.

She was in just to get her repeat prescriptions. I pulled one of the cardboard boxes out from under the chaise longue and looked for the folder with her name on it. It took some time, as Dr Rose appeared to have a poor grasp of the consecutive letters of the alphabet. When I eventually found her notes, I was none the wiser. Dr Rose obviously felt that he knew his patients so well that he could keep all his notes in his head. They were empty. I did find a reference to her appendix removal in 1946, but that was in a letter from the surgeon who had performed the operation.

'Och, it's a'richt, Doctor,' she reassured me. 'Ah ken whit Dr Rose gave me. It's a bottle of the white medicine and half a bottle of the green, and a few sweetie sleepers. Ye'll fin' them on that shelf there.'

On the shelf above the doctor's desk were the bottles of pills and boxes of creams and inhalers that formed the practice dispensary. By far the largest jar contained thousands of small oblong capsules, green at one end and red at the other, and a rather fetching mixed colour in the middle. I had no idea what they were. There was no label on the jar. I excused myself for a moment and went through the door into the main house, to seek Mrs Rose's help. She was sitting in the kitchen having an early morning coffee and a small glass of a golden liquid, the nature of which I didn't feel it was my place to enquire about. It was nine o'clock in the morning after all.

'Can you tell me what these are?' I asked her, proffering a few of the 'sweeties' in my hand. 'They are Tuinal,' she replied. 'Doctor often gave them to people to help them sleep. They help a lot. I take one or two a night myself.'

I returned to my patient. I had heard of Tuinal, but I'd never seen the pills in the flesh, so to speak. They were made up of a mixture of different types of barbiturate. Their makers claimed that they 'got people to sleep, kept them asleep, and let them wake up fresh each morning'. It certainly did the first two, but I had grave doubts on the third. In fact, Tuinal's real fame was for helping people not to wake up at all.

I settled down to have a serious chat with my patient, and for a few seconds thought I was getting somewhere with my lecture on the dangers of barbiturates. I might as well have talked to the wall. Her eyes had become glazed and fixed. It struck me that I was talking to someone who was virtually fast asleep, even though she was sitting on what must have been a most uncomfortable chair. I leaned forward and touched her forearm lightly. She stirred and apologised.

'I'm aye drapping aff like this in the mornings,'

she said. 'I cannae understaun it.'

I gently suggested it may have something to do with the Tuinal and added that it might be better for her to take it only on alternative nights for a while, to see if she wakened up a bit. I poured out her stomach medicine and her tonic and resolved to tackle why she was taking them at another visit.

She staggered out and I was glad to see on her notes that she lived a few yards away, on the same side of the road as the surgery, so she wouldn't be facing the danger of crossing it. I doubted whether she could have managed to cope with the kerb without falling over it. I walked to the greenhouse and called in the next patient...

By the end of the morning, I had seen around a dozen patients, nine of whom were on Tuinal, and all of whom were taking a combination of at least two of the three bottles. I never worked out the basis on which Dr Rose had chosen which combination for which patient. I suppose the reasons were lost in the mists of time: certainly the patients were of no help. They thought that as the good doctor had prescribed them, they must be doing them good. None of them, apparently, was ill. They all assumed that their good health was in no small measure due to Dr Rose's marvellous medicines.

Mrs Rose offered me a cup of tea after the surgery ended, then asked when she should order the next lot of medicines. It was a dispensing practice, which meant that the doctor not only prescribed the medicines but gave them out, too. The stores of medicines were replenished each week by an old pharmacist friend of Dr Rose, who saved him from having to worry about the details of ordering and maintaining his stocks. Dr Rose's main aim in life had been to keep his patients as happy as possible with the minimum of grief. Perhaps he had gone a little far by turning many of them into walking zombies, but it gave them, and him, particularly, a good night's sleep.

Mrs Rose was a decent lady, who took little interest in the running of the practice. She was looking forward to a quiet retirement with her sister, who was coming to stay. She wasn't sure that the friendly pharmacist would continue to supply the drugs, because he now wanted to retire, too, but she mentioned that Dr Renton, who had been the last doctor in the Braehill practice, had given her his dispensing records to give to me. I gathered later that he had not left them with Jeanie in Braehill, because she had a sharp brain and a keen interest in the doings of the doctors. Mrs Rose, on the other hand, was safe on two counts: she was a doctor's widow and knew when to be discreet, and she wasn't in the slightest bit interested in the running of the practice or his finances.

Mrs Rose suggested that I might like to take a leaf out of Dr Renton's book, as he seemed to have been very efficient at dispensing. She didn't know much about modern drugs, she said, but her one brief glance at Dr Renton's prescription profits suggested that he was more adept at organising things than her husband. And he certainly seemed to have earned more than her husband had.

I opened Dr Renton's ledger. He had made quite a profit from dispensing – in fact more than his salary. In a dispensing practice, the doctor would write out a prescription for each item dispensed. At the end of the month, all the prescriptions were sent to the Pricing Bureau, and the doctor received for each prescription a dispensing fee, the usual cost of the materials and a proportion of extra money added on as profit. The cheaper he could buy the pills and potions, the bigger would be the difference between his actual cost and the one estimated for the relevant drug by the Pricing Bureau. I looked at the dispensing records from the last few months and the totals from the Pricing Bureau. Dr Renton had worked hard, but within the law, to enhance his income. He had bought in 'generics' at low prices and claimed for them under their generic names. He had received the 'mark-up' that the Pricing Bureau thought was appropriate, based on the Bureau's estimate of cost. That was much higher than had actually been paid for the drugs, so his profit was a healthy one and still strictly according to the rules.

Dr Renton may have managed this strictly within the rules, but the whole area of prescribing and dispensing drugs offered less scrupulous doctors considerable room for fraud. In my former practice in Birmingham, it had been rumoured that Dr Dai had his own special prescription list. I never caught him actually doing it, but he would allegedly write 'tabs ADT, one daily' on the prescription and instruct the patient to go to his friendly pharmacist for it. The pharmacist would dispense something harmless and very cheap, such as a small dose of folic acid, or one of the B vitamins. At the end of each month, Dr Dai and the pharmacist would get together. The doctor would review all the ADT prescriptions and re-write them for something more expensive, such as an antibiotic or an anti-arthritis preparation. That prescription would be sent to the Pricing Bureau, and the pharmacist would glean a healthy profit, which would be split down the middle with Dr Dai.

Dr Dai's partner, Dr Owen, who declined to be 'on the take', did warn me about the ADT scam. Little wonder that I could not find 'Tabs ADT' in my *National Formulary*: it stood for 'any damn thing'.

As I drove back to the cottage from Collintrae that day, I realised that I had some hard decisions to make. The dispensing for Collintrae and Braehill had to be organised properly and we had to find, very urgently, a new place to consult in the village. Mairi and I also had to find a new home. As for the medication dished out ad lib from the surgery, I had to plan how to get most of the village population off Tuinal, and to discover what exactly was in those white, green and brown bottles.

The last was the easiest to achieve. Just after lunch, I had a phone call from Girvan. It was a social call: the town pharmacist, David Weir, a young man in his early thirties, was calling to welcome me to the district, and to offer any help I might need to get stocked with emergency and routine drugs. I jumped at the chance. I had no commitments that afternoon, so drove the fourteen miles into town to meet him. David told me that the mixtures were prepared by Dr Rose himself according to that old 1933 *Formulary*. We looked at the ingredients together. The white mixture was a simple antacid, a mixture of magnesium, aluminium and calcium carbonates, silicates and hydroxides. It would settle any stomach, but might well develop a concrete-like consistency in the bowel. I made a mental note to ask anyone who needed a repeat in the future about his or her toilet habits.

The green 'tonic' contained a large dose of *nux vomica*. The good people of Collintrae must have had strong stomachs, as even a smidgeon of *nux vomica* would make a newcomer to the medicine sick, and very quickly. Presumably the good doctor relied on the principle expounded by doctors from Hippocrates onwards that a 'medicine that can make you sick will stop you being sick'. The second part of that dictum is that 'once you get used to it, it will keep protecting you'. I didn't subscribe to either idea. All the notorious poisoners in history, from Lucrezia Borgia to 'Palmer the Poisoner' (a Victorian serial-killer GP), have relied on them for their success. *Nux vomica* isn't exactly arsenic or strychnine, but the principle isn't too different.

The *nux vomica* repeats would have to go. So would the brown medicine. It turned out to be a liquid version of 'Livingstone's rousers'. Every young man proceeding to Africa as a missionary, a diplomat or soldier in the nineteenth century was strongly advised to take several Livingstone's rousers every day. A mixture of rhubarb, jalap, calomel and quinine, it was designed to destroy any intestinal parasite known to the Victorian explorer and, in the passing, to take care of malaria, too. If the mixture didn't actually kill off the parasites, it made sure that food passed so quickly and in such a torrent from end to end that the poor microbes had no time to gain a foothold inside their host's gut. We were short of malaria cases, as far as I knew, in South Ayrshire, but I could see that the brown mixture would be a perfect, and perhaps the only, antidote to the white one. My only doubt was that the dose needed to dissolve the antacid concretion might be very close to that needed to dissolve the patient.

David and I liked each other straight off and have been firm friends ever since. He volunteered to help me organise my dispensing, and it went smoothly from that day on. I would add my small weekly order onto his much larger one, and I managed to dispense my prescriptions honestly and ethically, with no worries. I remain grateful to him for that to this day.

But what about the chloroform? As I drove home that afternoon, that remained a puzzle. It was solved that evening. I got a call from the Collintrae district nurse. There was a baby on the way to a Mrs Watson, in a farmhouse near the village. Could I join her?

I've always loved obstetrics, and I was excited to be

doing my first delivery in the district. This was Mrs Watson's third baby, the first two having been delivered at home by Dr Rose. The nurse, Flora Malcolm, was easing her into the third stage of labour, coaxing her and comforting her. I had the instant impression of an efficient, very professional, excellent colleague who could have delivered the baby standing on her head without my help. But in those days it was the doctor's job, and she moved aside for me. Mrs Watson watched me wash my hands in the basin and put on the gloves, and frowned a little.

'You won't put me out, Doctor? I'd like to be awake this time,' she said. Flora must have seen the surprise in my face. She explained: 'Dr Rose used to use chloroform just at the last, to help the baby out and ease the mother's pain. I presume we're going to do it differently now?'

'Sure,' I smiled at both of them and I spoke as reassuringly as I could to Mrs Watson. 'Maybe a little gas and air if you really need it, but we'd be glad to have you with us the whole way through it. Don't worry.'

It was a straightforward birth, a baby girl, and Mrs Watson said she would call her Flora after nurse, which brought a big beaming smile from the new namesake. Afterwards, Flora and I sat in my car outside the house, talking about the practice. Over the next few months, I found that she was as good as having another doctor on hand. She was as relieved as I was to lose the chloroform, and I reassured her she would never have to smell it again in the district.

How wrong I was. Two days later, Flora was at our home, in the kitchen, helping Mairi with Catriona. It was a Saturday morning, and the surgery was not to start until ten o'clock, so we had about an hour to have a leisurely coffee together and talk over baby things and practice problems. We were interrupted by the phone ringing. On the other end was a very agitated lady, crying that her husband had collapsed in the byre. Not only that, but all the cows had collapsed, and there was a funny smell. Could I come at once?

Flora came with me. The farm was four miles away from our cottage, and we took five minutes to get there, whizzing past tractors and milk tankers on the way. We pulled up to the farmyard to witness an amazing sight. Alec Campbell, the farmer, a big man in his late fifties, was lying prostrate just inside the entrance to the cowshed. Inside the shed were eighty cows, all of them lying on their sides, fast asleep. The air was thick with the pungent smell of chloroform.

Flora and I bent over Alec. He was gently snoring.

More than that, he was anaesthetised, but as far as we could see, otherwise well. We pulled him over to the house door, and let him lie there in the fresher air. The byre atmosphere was still permeated by the chloroform which, weirdly, appeared to be emanating from the cows. In danger of being chloroformed ourselves, we left the cows to themselves and started to tend to Alec. He came round quite quickly now that he was breathing fresh air.

It took us about ten minutes to understand what had happened. Alec was what might be called 'careful' with his money. He had a thousand sheep on his hill, along with his eighty milking cows. During the winter, the vet had found liver fluke in some of his sheep, and had advised Alec to dose them against the disease. Liver flukes are parasites that sheep pick up while grazing grass in which there are infected snails. The snails pass the parasite onto the grass, the sheep eat the grass, and the parasites find a cosy home inside the sheep's liver. An affected sheep fails to thrive, and that's a big loss in a herd of a thousand.

So Alec had ordered thousands of doses of the liver fluke antidote, carbon tetrachloride. Most people know of carbon tetrachloride from its use in the past as a dry-cleaning fluid – it's what gave dry-cleaning shops

82

their smell. It is a very efficient fluke killer, and for sheep it comes in handy little red oily capsules. The trick is to open the sheep's mouth and blow the capsule down its throat with an instrument like a peashooter.

Alec and his son Chris were adept at doing this. They dosed their thousand sheep over two or three days, and felt it was a job well done. But they were left with a thousand doses to spare, and didn't want to waste their money. The natural thing was to dose the cows, too. The cows shared the same pasture, and although they didn't show any signs of fluke, it was better to be safer than sorrier, wasn't it?

Unfortunately, Alec and Chris had made two mistakes in coming to this decision. The first was that they didn't know the dose to give the cows, and had assumed that it went by the weight of the animal. As a cow weighed about six times as much as a sheep, they decided to give each cow around six times the sheep's dose, which meant putting six capsules in the peashooter and blowing them in: dairy cows are surprisingly compliant about such interference, provided they are familiar with the man who does it.

The second mistake was not to read the instructions on the packets of capsules. When you are dosing hundreds of animals, it's easier to pour out all the capsules into a big container and take them from that when needed, so out with the old packaging went the instructions, too.

The label (which luckily Flora had retrieved from the farm bin) stated in large letters DO NOT GIVE TO ANIMALS FEEDING ON CONCENTRATES. Sheep graze on hillside grass. Concentrates are not within their rather narrow life horizon. On the other hand, cows find concentrates delicious: they help them produce more milk and keep them fat and happy. All of Alec's cows had been happily munching on concentrated feeds for the whole of their relatively contented lives. Of course, they liked variety, too, so the grass in the meadow was just as delicious, infected snails or not.

So why should a simple combination of dry-cleaning fluid and concentrates have such a surprising result? Here is a little chemistry lesson. When cows digest concentrated foods in their stomach, one of the by-products is hydrogen gas. Forty years on, the green-house gases, particularly methane and carbon dioxide, produced by belching cows, would worry the whole world. At that time, Flora and I and Mrs Campbell had another gas to worry about, however.

The chemical structure of carbon tetrachloride is simple: its name shows that a molecule contains one atom of carbon and four of chlorine. What happens when it meets up with hydrogen gas, released from the digestion of concentrates? One of the chlorine atoms is replaced by a hydrogen atom. That creates the compound carbon hydrogen trichloride. Its other name is chloroform.

Within minutes of swallowing such a whacking dose of carbon tetrachloride, each cow had started to manufacture chloroform in her stomach. It's not very far from the stomach to the lungs, and from there into the brain. Just as Alec was dosing his last cow, the first one to be dosed keeled over, with a loud clatter. As he rushed up to the unconscious animal, he was faced with cows going down like a stack of dominoes. One by one his precious cows fell over in their stalls. As they did so, they breathed out their chloroform into the air of the byre. Standing in the middle, Alec was getting the full benefit of the exhalations of eighty cows, all sound asleep. He joined them very soon afterwards.

Alec and his cows all recovered, although he wasn't allowed to send his milk to market until there was no more detected chloroform in it. Flora and I never found out who spilled the beans to the rest of the community. It certainly wasn't either of us, but forever afterwards his friends called him 'Chloroform Campbell'.

Chapter Six
Keepers and Poachers

As the first few weeks passed, Mairi and I settled in. We heard the rumours that the doctor 'was ower young' for the practice, and 'that wee wifie o' his is only eighteen (she was all of twenty-three) – they winna last.' But we bore them in good stead. Frankly the work was far less arduous than it had been in Birmingham and it was quality, rather than quantity, that mattered. I could spend a lot longer with each patient, and had time to smell the roses.

Roses there were, in fact, in plenty as the cottage was surrounded by them. They had been planted by the nuns years before, and made the cottage an ideal place to bring up a baby in the spring and early summer. I also had time to get to know our next-door neighbours, the lurching Archie and his long-suffering wife Agnes, extremely well. Too well, in fact, because we heard almost every word of their frequent rows across the open courtyard between us. Archie, being an outdoor type, tended to leave all the doors of their cottage open. We knew when things were brewing up badly when we heard the strains of "The Star of Rabbie Burns" drifting across to us. Archie fancied himself as a singer, and the more he drank, the more he fancied his own voice, and the more amorous he would become. Not unnaturally Agnes's own index of amorousness was in exact inverse proportion to Archie's. If there was one thing that turned her off him, it was that tune.

Archie was not the world's most attractive man – he was unshaven, a stranger to the bathroom or shower, and tended to wear, all the time, the clothes in which he had killed various vermin. 'Vermin' for Archie extended well beyond the usual rats, foxes and birds of prey that were the legitimate targets of his fellow gamekeepers. They included the neighbourhood's pet cats and small dogs, and Archie was adept not only at catching and dispatching them, but at hiding their bodies so that his mass murder would not be detected by the rest of the villagers, who were mystified by the regular disappearance of their pets. Rumour had it that there was a large predator in the woods around the village, perhaps one of those big black cats, like a panther, that had been seen from time to time in a forest further north.

I didn't doubt for a second that Archie was the 'panther': during our chats in the yard behind our cottages he explained his calling to me. It was his job to produce as many pheasants as possible for each autumn's shoot, and any animal, cat, dog, fox or man who dared to meddle with that would face his retribution. I never saw him with any mantraps, but I had no doubt that he would use one if he felt the need. He generally made do with vicious 'pole' traps, which he would set on top of gate posts and bait with small portions of meat. As the bird settled on the pole to take the meat it sprung the trap, and two iron-toothed jaws would close on the unfortunate animal's torso, crushing it to death. He caught owls, kestrels, falcons and even buzzards like this. Hares and cats he caught in similar traps set in their 'runs' in the undergrowth, and rabbits he caught in snares. You had to be very careful walking through the woods that Archie tended.

He had his good side: when he was sober he taught me the rudiments of fly fishing in the burn just in front of the cottages. I still have the small black-and-white photograph of the first trout I caught, and Archie grinning beside me. He reasoned that if I could be introduced to country sports I would be his ally in the never-ending fight against his enemies. It didn't work out that way.

Agnes was a very different person. Where Archie was overweight and ruddy-faced, the result of his constant exposure to the wind, the sun and alcohol, Agnes was thin and cowed, face pale and lined well beyond her years. Her eyes were still bright, though, and anyone could see that she had been, when younger, a good-looking woman. I was astonished to see from her medical notes that she was only thirty-seven: she looked fifty or more. She dressed as cleanly and neatly as she could on the meagre amount she was given after Archie had drunk most of the wages. There was always a pot of soup on the stove made from the vegetables she had grown in the small garden, with a piece of rabbit or hare, provided by Archie, thrown in 'for a wee taster'. She would share that soup with anyone, despite her very limited means, provided they stayed and talked a while afterwards.

The day after we arrived, Agnes walked into our cottage kitchen with a big, steaming pot of her soup. I'd never tasted anything so delicious. She beamed when I asked for a little more, then turned her attention to Catriona – her real reason, I'm sure, for coming in. She and Archie hadn't been able to have children themselves, she said, and she just loved babies.

Mairi gave her Catriona to hold. Agnes beamed again, holding the baby to her breast and, swaying gently, looked down at Catriona's sleeping face.

'When was she born?' she asked.

'The Ides of March – the thirteenth,' I replied.

'No, Doctor,' she said, in a way that gently chided me for my inaccuracy. 'The Ides of March are on the fifteenth. Just as they are in May, July and October. It's on the other months that they're on the thirteenth.'

I looked at her in a new light. Here was a woman, as poor as there could be in Britain, teaching me about the Roman calendar. It turned out that she had done well in the village school and had loved the classics. The old head teacher, Clunie MacPherson, who still lived in the village, told me later that Agnes had been one of the brightest pupils he had ever taught. She could easily have gone to university: instead, she had been forced to leave at fifteen to make her living as a maid in the 'big hoose'. Clunie had smiled ruefully at the thought of Agnes, with an IQ fifty points above anyone else in the house, wasting her life below stairs, cleaning, washing dishes and bringing in the coals and logs. The only available male in her life had been Archie, and she had jumped out of the frying pan of servitude into the fire of Archie's alcoholism and violence. It was a hard life, said Clunie. But once a week, he and Agnes, and a few older former pupils, still met to discuss philosophy and the classics in his small front room. That lightened her load a little, and made Clunie happy, too.

We didn't have Archie and Agnes as neighbours for long. Late one July evening, we heard a knock at the back door of the cottage. It was a boy I hadn't met before. Alan Gordon was eleven years old. He was small and wiry, with sunken cheeks and a wheeze I could hear clearly as he was standing a few feet in front of me. He plainly had asthma, but that wasn't what he had come for.

It was twilight, but in the glow from the kitchen behind me I could see he was pale and was grimacing with pain. He was clamping his right forearm firmly between his left upper arm and the side of his chest, hiding it from my view. He was on his own. He kept glancing towards the McLarens' cottage, as if he was afraid to be caught near it. It was then I noticed that he was shivering, violently, although the night wasn't frosty, and he was warmly dressed in a thick overcoat and long trousers tucked into his boots.

'You the doctor?' he asked.

'Yes,' I said, 'come on in and get warm. You look as if you are freezing.'

'I'm no cauld, Doctor, I'm just scared.'

He walked past me into the kitchen. I shut the door and he turned to face me. He took his hand from its hiding place. Clamped around his wrist were the jaws of a gin trap. It wasn't man-size, but it was certainly big enough to damage pretty severely the thin wrist of an eleven-year-old boy. Surprisingly, there was no bleeding.

I took him into the lounge, where Mairi was seated on a couch. I must say here that the last thing she had wanted to be was a nurse. Her subject at college had been hotel management, which was great training for running the business side of a family doctor's practice, but hardly appropriate when dealing with medical emergencies. Give her credit, she rose up and managed to clear a space on the couch for young Alan before she fainted clear away on the floor. I now had two casualties in the room – one a boy in shock (the cause of the shivering) and the other an unconscious woman lying on her back with her heels drumming out a steady beat on the wooden floor.

Alan was so concerned that he came instantly out of his shock. He forgot about the trap on his arm and stared at her.

'Whit's wrang wi' her? Is she havin' a fit?' he asked. 'Is it ma fault?'

'No, it's OK,' I said to him. 'She has only fainted. We will see to you first.'

Luckily, the trap hadn't been strong enough to break a bone, and the stiff cloth of his coat had stopped it from tearing the skin. I was able to prize the jaws of the trap open and relieve the pain. His wrist was bruised, but he could move his fingers and wrist normally.

'No real harm done,' I said to him, and we both turned to Mairi, who was groggily raising herself from the floor. She took a little longer than Alan to recover, and I went off into the kitchen to make a cup of tea for the three of us. I don't think any medicine has yet been devised that's better than hot sweet tea for shock or a faint.

Mairi and I took our time to get to know Alan that evening. He was one of five brothers and two sisters who lived with their parents in a council house in Kilminnel, just across the road from the village policeman. That was unfortunate for the Gordons, because they were not, to put it delicately, always on the side of the law.

That wasn't to say they were criminals exactly. They saw the taking of a few rabbits and hares from the large estates in the surrounding valleys as a form of pest control. The fact that the asinine laws of Scotland at the time stated that this was illegal didn't impinge on their ethical or moral feelings on the subject. Generations of Gordons had taken their meat where they could and had never harmed anyone in doing so. Alan was just following in the family tradition. So when he had put his hand down a rabbit burrow to check on the snare he had set there, it was a painful discovery to find a gin trap in its place.

Archie McLaren must have known about the burrow and the snare, and that his gin trap might cause severe injury to whoever had set it. I didn't like that at all. Alan had walked the four miles from Kilminnel to Braehill to tend his snares: I decided to take him home in my car, and talk to his parents about it.

They were happy to see us, and thanked me profusely for bringing Alan home. I told them I would support them if they wanted to bring charges against Archie: after all, gin traps of any kind were now outside the law, and setting one where a child, poacher or not, could be trapped by it was unacceptable. They politely refused to take things further. No, the villagers around here do things in their own way, they said, McLaren will learn his lesson.

And learn he did, the hard way. The last weeks of July are crucial for pheasants. It's the time when the new season's chicks are big enough to be set free from the pens in which they are reared. Pheasants are particularly stupid birds: they will walk anywhere without a care in the world. It's impossible in the Stinchar Valley in the late summer and the autumn not to come across dozens of them in the roads and hedgerows. I wonder sometimes if they commit suicide by running in front of cars just so they will miss being shot later.

If you are a gamekeeper, the only way you can guarantee to keep your pheasants around your own fields and woods is to keep feeding them grain in specific places, so that they always return, morning and night, to them. Archie had around a dozen of these places strategically placed in the shooting fields and hills. He would drive to them each morning and evening on weekdays to replenish the grain stocks. He was supposed to do so, too, on Fridays and Saturdays, but his fondness for John Barleycorn sometimes got in the way.

When word about what had happened to young Alan got about, plans were hatched. Archie had a few more enemies than he knew about in the village. There were those who were suspicious about their lost cats and others, including the storekeeper, to whom he owed money. They weren't exactly scared of him, but they were aware of his strength and his temper, and knew that picking an argument with him would end in violence. The Braehill and Kilminnel people are gentle folk – until spurred into action.

So it was that certain members of the two villages decided to treat Archie one Saturday evening to a few extra drinks. Archie was never averse to being treated: he was dimly aware that this was unusual, but reasoned that they might be wanting to bribe him for jobs as beaters when the shooting season started. That was fine by him.

Other villagers were on a stealthier mission. At each of the pheasant feeders they replaced the grain with corn they had specially prepared beforehand, laced liberally with whisky, that had been, how shall we say, 'manufactured' in a certain large copper vessel up in the hills above one of the villages. When Customs and Excise eventually found one of the bottles a few years later it was measured at one hundred and ten degrees proof.

It is a common belief that animals don't like alcohol. If laboratory rats are given the choice between alcohol-laden and alcohol-free food, we are told that they always choose the latter, unless they are put under severe stress.

Well, Archie's pheasants were either under severe stress, or the laboratory results do not extrapolate to pheasants in the wild. Once one pheasant had tasted the delicious new feed, it gave the clarion call to the others to share in its good fortune. Within minutes, all the pheasants for miles around were gobbling up the feed as if it were Christmas. Within an hour they were all doing a passable imitation of Archie, who at that moment was gently snoring on the padded bench in the back room of the Braehill Arms.

Avid readers who know their Paul Gallico may be reminded here of his story of drunken pheasants. It told of a man and his son who, having put out alcohol-soaked feed for the birds in a wood, waited until they had fallen off their perches in the trees before harvesting them from the ground. Archie's pheasants couldn't have made it to their perches – they were far too sozzled to attempt to fly. They stayed woozily on the ground, within yards of their feeding stations, until they fell asleep.

So it was simple for the men (and boys – I have heard, though of course I had no proof, that Alan and his brothers were among them) to pick the pheasants up and place them in the backs of their trucks. It is difficult for anyone who lives near a thousand pheasants to imagine how they could be transported silently through the night on open-backed trucks, but I am assured that that is exactly what happened. All that could be heard from them, it is said, were a few gentle snores, as the birds dreamed their night away.

The Kilminnel men could have sold their haul to hotels around Britain for a large profit. After all, the birds were already marinaded. But that wasn't the plan. They were not thieves and didn't, as far as anyone knows to this day, harm a single pheasant. Instead they picked a perfect spot from which the pheasants could be retrieved. Kilminnel Church has a walled garden beside it, in which there is plenty of room for a thousand pheasants to puddle about happily for a day or two, eating the wild grass and flower seeds, but with no chance of escape. It's said that they took a day or so to get over their hangovers and to be able to walk with some sense of balance again.

The minister was amazed to see them all on the Sunday morning, as were the country folk from the 'big hoose', Archie's employers, as they walked up to the church door for the morning service. Minister and laird alike had no idea how the pheasants had got there. Nor did they know whose pheasants they were, at least until

'The minister was amazed to see them all on the Sunday morning, as were Archie's employers, as they walked up to the church door for the morning service.'

after the church service, which was unusually well attended that morning. Could it possibly have been that people wanted to see the laird's face when the truth dawned? Surely not.

Archie woke later on that morning to a worse than usual Sunday hangover, and to an irate landowner who wanted to know why his land was empty of any evidence of pheasant life and smelled like a distillery, and why the minister appeared now to have a thousand pheasants in his garden. Could there possibly be a link, and could Archie kindly provide it?

Of course, Archie couldn't. It was a nightmare from which he never recovered. It turned out to be much more difficult to move the now sober and hyperactive pheasants back to their home, and the numerous helpful offers of special grain to calm them down seemed somehow to enrage him further. He couldn't face the future in Braehill. He and Agnes left for pastures new a few weeks later. Except we heard that they weren't pastures, but a city flat where the views were of sandstone, bricks and mortar and where no pheasant, drunk or sober, ever showed its plumage.

We were sad to lose Agnes, but we heard later that she had become the breadwinner. Clunie still had some influence in educational circles. Agnes won a university bursary, and after pursuing her studies further, went on to become first a lecturer and then a reader in classics. She has written books on philosophy that are beyond me. I presume she left Archie far behind.

As for the new gamekeeper, the laird had to make a fast decision. He was in the middle of the pheasant-rearing season and had to fill the job quickly. So he gave it to Alan's dad Callum, on the basis that a poacher would know the ropes. Alan became his apprentice, and I've watched him and his children grow up, spending as much time taking visitors and birders around their far-flung parts of Scotland, pointing out the birds of prey, and showing them the red squirrels, the otters and pine martens, as they do rearing pheasants.

CHAPTER SEVEN
CLUNIE'S CLOCKS

After having met Agnes I was curious to meet her mentor, Clunie. In those days in country practice, doctors had a monthly visit list for all their 'elderly frail'. It's a part of practice that I much regret has been lost in the last few years. As workloads have expanded, visits have taken a back seat. It is more efficient to bring people into the surgery. We can see six people an hour that way, against two an hour when visiting. Efficiency is today's mantra, but it's a mantra for those who didn't experience the old ways of doing things. We have lost a lot, in 2007, by building all practice around the surgery, and not around the home.

To get back to my first visit to Clunie. He lived in a

beautiful stone house set in a well-tended garden just at the beginning of Braehill village. Built in the 1890s, when the boom in woollens and mohair had made the village prosperous, it had the living space for a large family and two or three servants. Clunie lived in it alone, but he wasn't in the least lonely.

He had all his family around him. There were his parents, grandparents and five maiden aunts. Obviously they weren't alive; they were in oil paintings and alabaster busts, in fading photographs and in framed embroidery. There were mountains of books, diaries, and letters in blocks bound in ribbons. There were also three pianos, two cellos, three sofas, half a dozen leather armchairs and the same number again covered in velvet. The chairs and sofas bore pristine, creaseless, lace-trimmed white antimacassars. There were three dining tables, several writing desks and two legal partners' desks. The floor was thick with carpets, laid one on top of another. The upper ones had obviously been made to measure for other rooms, as their edges and corners didn't fit: intriguing glimpses of even finer carpets showed below the ones Clunie and his guests walked on.

Then there were the clocks. In each room there were two or three grandfather and grandmother clocks, and on every table and desk were collections of mantel clocks, carriage clocks, and clocks in glass cases or gilt cases with rotating balls or swinging pendula. There were old circular railway station clocks on the walls of three of the rooms. They were all at the right time. Once, when I visited him around noon, those that could strike out the twelve hours did so. It was like having an orchestra of glockenspiels in the house.

This was all on the ground floor. I never did find out what was upstairs, because the staircase was filled with Victorian and Edwardian bric-à-brac. There were piles of cases, boxes, books, crockery and vases all the way up to the landing. You couldn't have gone up the stairs if you tried. It was difficult enough to walk into the front room from the front door: you first had to wend your way between two gigantic Chinese vases, then between stools, chairs, standard lamps, music stands and piles of clothes. Once in the front room, it was tricky to place your feet one after another without stepping on some precious ornament. Clunie must have held his meetings with Agnes and her friends in the kitchen, the only room in which it was possible to sit.

He lived in his ground-floor bedroom, in which there was a large four-poster bed complete with its cloth canopy, hanging drapery around the sides and roped curtains around the four corners. He was seated, on that first visit, in an easy chair, one of the leather ones. A small, wiry man, he had a flowing white beard that covered his neck. He was immaculate, with not a button missing or a stain in sight. His clothes were like his furniture, around seventy years out of fashion. A green and yellow embroidered smoking cap complete with tassel covered his balding head. He wore a matching green velvet smoking jacket, with a silk shirt and a yellow cravat, perfectly tied. Moleskin trousers in darker green and soft green slippers completed the look.

He apologised for not getting up to greet me: his legs didn't work as well as they used to. He had already heard about me from Agnes, he said, and was looking forward to a chat or two over the weeks to come. Nodding towards a crystal decanter on the sideboard, just within arm's reach of his chair, he asked me to join him in a glass of port. I could hardly refuse, and poured a generous tot for him and a smaller one for myself. I sat on the side of his bed – the only other suitable place to sit in the room – and we started talking. I didn't get away for more than an hour.

Clunie had been the only child of a father who had been killed in the Boer War, and a mother who had died shortly afterwards of a 'broken heart'. To judge from her collections of crystal decanters and the oil paintings that

105

showed her with a complexion on the yellow side, the broken organ might in fact have been her liver. He had then been brought up by his mother's sisters, the five maiden aunts, all of them schoolteachers. In those times, he explained, if women teachers got married they had to give up their jobs. His aunts had preferred their careers to any man they might have met, so they stayed single. Consequently, as they died, one by one in old age, their precious belongings had been left to him. Which was how the contents of five Edwardian households had come to be stuffed into his one house.

Clunie was a sentimental man. He didn't like to throw anything away, especially not mementoes of his beloved aunts. That explained all the furniture and the bric-à-brac, but it didn't explain the one set of items in the room that was completely out of character. The bed had only three legs. The fourth leg must have broken off many years before, because that corner of the bed was held in place by a pile of extremely thick books. Dust had coated them over the years, but I could see that the one in the middle had a bright red cover, with *Medical Directory 1888* written in gold letters across its spine. I bent over a little to read the titles of the others, which were of much duller hues, bound as they were in fading leather.

Clunie noticed my interest and smiled. 'You are interested in old medical books?'

I nodded and screwed my eyes up to read the fading print on the books. 'Then you can have them when I'm dead,' he said. 'I need them for now to hold up my bed.'

They were an expensive bed support. Apart from the *Medical Directory*, there were two volumes of the *Dictionary of Practical Surgery* edited by Christopher Heath FRCS, *Diseases of the Ear and Naso-Pharynx* by Hovell, two volumes of *The Science and Art of Surgery* by Erichsen, and *Hooper's Medical Dictionary*, obviously from its binding and print style a much older book. How do I remember them so well? They are on the shelf above my desk as I write. Each book is signed on the fly-leaf by Clunie's grandfather, 'H. MacPherson, 1887'.

Hugh MacPherson had qualified in 1875 from Glasgow. He had married young, and with a son to care for, he needed a rural practice to make sure that he had good healthy air to breathe. Braehill was perfect. The *Medical Directory* revealed a population in the three villages of more than 10,000, compared to the 1,850 in 1964 and the 1,400 of today. Rural depopulation continues as I write.

In Dr MacPherson's time there were enough people in the area to support six doctors – two in Braehill, two in Kilminnel and two in Collintrae. When young Hugh arrived in Braehill, an older doctor had died, and the remaining one was keen to grab all the loot that he could.

'The story goes,' said Clunie, 'that old Dr Kinnaird would have nothing to do with my grandfather. He had objected to him coming and put up all sorts of barriers to him staying. Then one day, my grandfather fell into the river when crossing it to see a patient on a winter's night. He was injured and cold – what I suppose you might call hypothermia today. Dr Kinnaird refused to treat him, despite my grandmother's pleading, and my grandfather died the next day. He was just thirty-seven, with a fourteen-year-old son – my father. My grandmother was heartbroken, but stayed on in Braehill, with sympathy from everyone. The villagers rallied round, and all Dr Kinnaird's patients left him for one of the Kilminnel doctors. So he had to leave Braehill shortly afterwards.

'My father joined the army and married the girl next door. Within a year I was born, and within another year, *they* were both dead – him in South Africa, her here. I was brought up by my grandmother and my mother's sisters. I went from one aunt to the next and, as they were all schoolteachers, I learned a lot from them. I taught classics at university for a while but, when my grandmother took ill, I applied for the post of teacher at Braehill School, and have been here ever since.'

'You never married?' I ventured, wondering if I was overstepping the mark and prying too deeply into what was then a very private area for any man, especially an Edwardian one.

'I was never really interested in women,' he said, then added with a laugh, 'and not in men, either, if that's what you are hinting at.' He was in his late sixties, and I remember thinking how much older than that he looked.

'So how are you?' I asked, remembering why I was there. 'Have you any problems?'

'It's just a wee problem with my legs,' he answered. I had noticed when I saw him first that his ankles were a little swollen, and had wondered about his heart: his cheeks were more of a dusky blue than a country red. I helped him take his slippers off, and with a sinking heart saw that his swollen feet were nearer black than blue. They weren't painful – not a good sign. Nor was the fact that, when I pressed a finger into the top of his foot, the depression it made stayed like a dimple in the skin. He was in heart failure, and the circulation in the legs was blocked. It wouldn't be long before they were gangrenous.

Clunie was dying of the complications of poorly controlled diabetes. He had never been able to follow a diet or curb his fondness for good port and wine, or his meerschaum pipe which he filled several times a day with thick black tobacco. Now he was paying the price.

He must have seen my face as I sat up.

'You don't have to tell me, Doc. I'm not stupid. But I want to stay here for as long as I can.'

I promised that I would help as much as I could. Jane Forrest, the Braehill district nurse, Flora's counterpart in this end of the practice, would come in more often, and we would do what we could to make him comfortable. There were plenty of volunteer ladies in the village, most of them ex-pupils, who would gladly give their time to keep him company and comfortable.

He passed away in his sleep, three weeks later, as far as I knew with no distress. He must have been aware that his death was imminent, however, because he had left a note on the pillow beside his head.

'The State can have my effects,' it read, 'but the medical books under my bed are to go to Dr Smith.'

I have them now, still in front of me, beside my twenty-first-century state-of-the-art computer, just to remind me of a really good man and his grandfather.

But that's not the end of Clunie's story. In Scotland, when someone dies with no relatives and no will, a lawyer is appointed to hold a sale of his possessions, the proceeds going to the Crown. Mairi and I, still starting out in our married life, and about to move into our first substantial home in Collintrae, were interested in some of the furniture, and perhaps one of the grandmother clocks. So we decided to go to the sale.

It was run by Wallace Brundell, senior partner of E., J. and R. Brundell & Sons, lawyers. E., J. and R. had died years before, leaving Wallace, a grandson of E. and son of J., as sole lawyer. R. had been an uncle. Their law practice was based in Darley, a small mining town around six miles to the east of Girvan. I phoned the office to find the place of the sale. Asking for Mr Brundell, I was told by a lady clerk that there was no need to speak to the man himself: a notice would be in the local paper shortly. She sounded snooty to say the least. I mentioned the note about the books, and was sharply informed that it did not have any standing in law, and that I would have to bid for them like anyone else. The phone was put down abruptly: clearly I had no business taking up her precious time.

The notice eventually appeared two days before the sale. It was to be held in Mr Brundell's own warehouse, all the effects having been removed from Clunie's house a few days before. There had been little opportunity for anyone to browse around.

Mairi and I arrived an hour before the start. We were astonished to find just a few pieces of furniture, sad and worn, in an almost empty hall. The busts, pictures, desks, tables, vases, musical instruments, chairs, lamps, ornaments and all the valuable items that Clunie had cared for so lovingly were nowhere to be seen. Where could they be?

I asked the auctioneer, a tall, sombre man in a dark suit and plain tie. He had sleeked-down black hair and a thin face with pince-nez tightly gripping his aquiline nose. He brushed my question aside. He did not understand how I could have thought that Mr MacPherson had a house full of treasures. These few things were all that had been taken out of the house. He was well known to be a recluse, and he could hardly have had much, being just a village schoolmaster. Now could he get on with the auction, please?

I got the message. Someone was on the take, and it would be impossible to prove who that person was. I was sure the auctioneer was in on it, but had no evidence to make any accusation. The little pile of medical books was there – but none of the others. I got the feeling that after my conversation with the clerk in Brundell's office, she had told the boss that the books had better be in the auction. I bid a pound for them. No one else made a bid, so I picked up my books, handed over the pound, and Mairi and I left, disappointed not just because we hadn't had the chance to buy anything really worthwhile, but also because we thought that Clunie and his ancestors had in some way been cheated.

A week later, just before midnight on a Thursday, the Girvan police called me. Could I come at once to a house in Darley? There had been a sudden death. Here I must explain that the Collintrae and Darley doctors had an arrangement. Darley was a mining town, with a single-handed doctor, Arthur Thomson, running a busy mixed practice of farming and mining families. Arthur and I had one night a week off duty. I took Wednesday off, Arthur took Thursday. We stood in for each other on those nights, so that one night a week we looked after two practices. To balance the one busy night, we could guarantee at least one night a week in which we wouldn't be disturbed. We really appreciated that and thought the double duty was worth it.

So I was happy to drive the fifteen miles to Darley, but puzzled by the call. When I had asked how the patient had died, the policeman had said that I would see when I got there. I wasn't sure, but I thought I had heard a laugh in the background when he said it. I couldn't think how laughter could be appropriate when dealing with a sudden death, although even now I can't help a wry smile when I think about it.

I drove up the drive of the most imposing house. In small towns like this such a house was either the minister's or the doctor's. I knew it wasn't the doctor's. Arthur and his wife Eve lived in a modest house next to the surgery, and this one was at the posher end of the town. It wasn't the manse, either, as the church was several streets away. I was told later that it had been built many years before by the mine owner, whose fortune and interest in the village had evaporated when the mines were nationalised.

As the policeman at the door let me in, it dawned on me that it must be the house of the only other person of note in any small town – the lawyer. I walked along the hall, passing the open door of the front room, where a woman in a white nightdress was being comforted by the minister. Hearing her voice, I recognised it as that of the 'clerk' on the lawyer's phone.

I was shown upstairs into a bedroom. Fortunately for the woman, the couple slept in twin beds. The bed-clothes on the nearer one were thrown back, the sheet rumpled as if someone had been in bed and got out in a hurry. The second bed was still occupied. The man was lying on his back. I could see his face, calm and peaceful as is every dead person's face, no matter how he or she has died. I get impatient with those detective stories in which the victims' faces are distorted in terror after death. The muscles of the face relax after death, so that it is expressionless. The eyes remain open, so that it is different from sleep, but there is never a hint in the face of whether the person felt pain or surprise when they breathed their last.

Which is why the man in the bed didn't show surprise or alarm or pain, even with two grandfather clocks, a large bust of Clunie's Aunt Ethel and a marble pillar on top of him. His eyes were fixed on the gaping hole in the ceiling through which they had fallen, but whether he had had time to see them fall is impossible to say.

I looked carefully at the face. There was the high forehead, the sleeked-back hair, the marks of the pince-nez on the aquiline nose. He looked friendlier in death than when I had last met him at the auction.

One of the policemen helped me to move the clocks, the bust and the pillar. The auctioneer's face may have been unmarked, but the rest of him was a mess. This isn't

'...two grandfather clocks, a large bust of Clunie's Aunt
Ethel and a marble pillar on top of him. His eyes were
fixed on the gaping hole in the ceiling... but whether he
had had time to see them fall is impossible to say.'

a medical book, so I won't go into the gory details, but human ribs and internal organs aren't built to resist several hundred kilos of hardwood and marble falling from around twelve feet above them.

I hadn't realised when I met him at the sale that the auctioneer was in fact also the lawyer – Mr Brundell. I had assumed that the lawyer would employ a professional auctioneer to do the selling. In hindsight, of course, it was obvious that he had to do it all himself – to get trusted men to pick up the stuff, then store it in as safe a place as possible until he could find a way to sell it on, perhaps at an auction house miles away. Where better could he hide it but in his own roof space? There were stairs into it and he and his wife, with perhaps a helper, could have done it easily.

He hadn't taken into account the age of the house and the parsimony of the mine owner who had built it a century before. Never a man to pay his workers well, the mine man had obviously carried that principle into his dealings with his builders. They had responded, probably unknown to him, by skimping on the hidden parts of the house – like the roof timbers and loft flooring. Add a little damp rot over the years, and there was no chance that they could support extra weight. The marble and mahogany were far too much for them to bear.

The Procurator Fiscal's inquiry held a few months later recorded a verdict of accidental death. Auntie Ethel may have had something to do with it. The pathologist found that her bust had broken the ribs on the left side of his chest, rupturing his heart as it did so.

The police found the rest of Clunie's treasures in the part of the loft that hadn't given way. I was asked to identify what I could, as the person who had most recently seen them in situ. They were confiscated as 'evidence' and later sold at an auction in Edinburgh, at prices many times those that would have been paid in Darley. Mairi and I don't have any other Clunie mementoes, but the books are enough.

CHAPTER EIGHT
A SOCIAL WHIRL

Before Collintrae, I was pretty much a stranger to social evenings. There were plenty of reasons for this. Young doctors then were only really admitted to polite society as they moved up the ladder of medical seniority. And parties in the hospital mess – where the junior doctors met – certainly didn't train us for the outside world. Our meagre eight pounds a month didn't stretch to entertaining or being entertained. We were limited to the local beer generously donated to the mess by nearby breweries.

Nor were we senior enough for anyone to ask us our opinion on anything, so we were never included in the consultants' social whirls. As a result our conversation was severely limited, because we knew nothing about anything other than medicine.

But as soon as we hit the registrar grade in hospital or became GPs, the scene changed. We began to be invited to various grand parties and social evenings where we met, often for the first time since we had started our studies, people from other walks of life. It wasn't easy at first. We had moved in one quick step from the lowest status of all, students – which father wants his precious offspring to date a medical student? – to one of the highest. Who doesn't want his daughter to marry a doctor?

Several weeks after our arrival, Mairi and I were sent a gold-embossed card from the local titled landowner. Could we grace his home with our presence at a party the following week?

We were flattered, and on the evening dressed, as we thought, fittingly for the event. Naturally, I was the only one there wearing a lounge suit. Everyone else, having noted in the corner of the invitation 'black tie', was in full dinner regalia. Not that it mattered particularly. It did not take me long to realise that the parish minister and I were there not for our scintillating conversation or sartorial panache, but as the representatives of our respective callings and our status in country society. As for the other guests, their purpose that evening was, it seemed, to get smashed, preferably as fast as possible.

As I was still on call I couldn't join them, so I resigned myself to the role of wallflower, watching the inevitable descent into chaos unfold. Mairi and I teamed up with the minister and his wife, sadly not the most riveting of companions, to make an awkward foursome in an unobtrusive corner, sipping orange juice and ginger ale.

It wasn't long before I had to put my medical knowledge into action. High heels, a threadbare stair carpet and a stomach full of pink gin combined to cause a female guest to trip and twist an ankle. She lay on the bottom stair, moaning gently and holding her foot. Various semi-drunken and some frankly fully-drunken gentlemen and ladies offered their services, until our hostess interrupted them with, 'There is a doctor here, would someone fetch him?'

One of the waitresses hired for the evening was a patient of mine, so she came over to us and grinned at me.

'Milady would like you to come into the hall, please, Doctor. One of the ladies needs your attention,' she said. Then, whispering, 'I don't think it'll be the last time tonight.'

The crowd parted like the Red Sea as I approached the casualty. A quick feel of the swollen ankle confirmed that it was simply a sprain. I asked 'milady' for some ice and a bandage. There was plenty of ice – it was in buckets placed in every room, cradling bottles of wine. Bandages took a little longer. Milady needed to ask the butler where they might be. Milord, naturally, had no idea and was already, only an hour or so into the evening, in no fit state to find them.

As I set to work organising a cold compress and a firm bandage, I could hear the conversation around me. Kensington mixed with Morningside as their subject switched from local gossip to the competence of 'this man' bending over their friend. My mixture of Birmingham and Glasgow – not an accent they would have heard much – obviously unsettled them.

'Can we trust him?' said a female voice with clipped BBC tones. 'After all, what would a decent doctor be doing in a backwater like this?'

'Of course you can trust him,' came another female voice, this time a soft Highland one. I grinned to myself.

'He is a brilliant doctor. You couldn't have a better one,' the voice continued. It was Mairi's.

Milady was nothing if not direct.

'How do you know it's just a sprain?' she asked me.

'Shouldn't it be X-rayed, just in case it's broken?'

I counted to ten under my breath, then showed her – and the gaggle of interested bystanders around us – how I diagnosed the sprain.

'If it were broken,' I answered, 'it would hurt when I squeeze here or if I thump the sole of her foot.'

I squeezed her anklebones together and thumped the sole of her foot. My patient did not yelp.

'If it is sprained, it will hurt if I twist the outside of the foot downward, like this.'

I twisted it downward. She yelped, quite loudly. My point was made quite well, I thought, but not entirely to the patient's satisfaction.

'So how do you treat a sprain?' Milady was persistent.

I continued my bandaging.

'Just remember RICE,' I said. 'Rest, Ice, Compression and Elevation. You bind the joint in ice, quite tightly, raise the foot to above body level, and leave it there for twenty-four hours. The patient can start to walk the day after that.'

When I finished the bandaging, two large men lifted the afflicted guest to a nearby sofa, where she spent the rest of the party ordering more drinks. She seemed to take very well to lying on her back with her legs on the armrest, so I assumed she was used to the position.

I took a sip of my dry ginger ale, and watched as an older man weaved his way towards me. I groaned inwardly. He was a typical 'spot diagnosis'. At medical school we would have 'spot' sessions, in which the students sat in a row, and patients were asked to walk in front of us, entering the room by one door and leaving by another without uttering a sound. Our task was to note any abnormalities in their looks or their gait that would betray their underlying disease, and write down the most likely answer on a note pad. It was a popular class: we saw twenty patients in about ten minutes, and after a dozen sessions or more we became experts at 'spotting'.

This man was flushed, shaking, bleary-eyed, unsteady, and carried a large glass the same colour as mine in his left hand. It wasn't ginger ale. He used a stick to lean on with his right.

'I hear you're a quack,' he said. It was a bad start. Doctors don't like being called quacks, even in fun, at a party. 'Tell me,' he said, 'what's macrocytosis? My doctor says I have it, and it means I have to go off the booze. Do I really have to?'

This one is trouble, I thought.

'Well,' I said, 'it means your red cells are a lot

bigger than they should be.'

'What's that got to do with the booze?' he asked.

'It's a sign that your liver is giving up. It's not able to provide the right proteins to make normal cells. You are probably anaemic, too. Only giving up alcohol altogether will make it right.'

Then I took the plunge – probably unwisely.

'For a start, you shouldn't be drinking that,' I said, glancing at his glass. 'You are in deep trouble if you drink at all. You need to give your liver a total rest.'

'Pah,' he said. 'You quacks are all the same.'

He waved his glass at me. As it passed a few inches under my nose I caught the sweet smell of neat malt whisky. He swallowed a large mouthful.

'You always want to spoil a man's fun.'

Now that it was obvious that I wasn't a bearer of good news, he turned away and shambled off. I made to join the three other teetotal partygoers in the corner.

I didn't make it across the room. I felt a hand at my elbow. It was the lady of the house.

'Doctor, I'd like to thank you for looking after our guest. You did such a splendid job. I do hope you are enjoying yourself,' she said.

It's about the same as enjoying an average surgery, I thought, but I smiled, and said that I was.

'I wonder, however, if you would do me a great kind-ness,' she continued. 'Could I have a quiet word with you in the library?'

I looked across at Mairi, deep in conversation with the minister's wife. We glanced at each other, and a ghost of a smile flitted across her face. She knew what was happening.

'Lead the way,' I said.

I'd seen pictures of libraries like this in Agatha Christie films. Hercule Poirot or Miss Marple would sit in them, with all the suspects standing around, awaiting the dénouement nervously. The leather-bound books were floor to ceiling, with a wrought iron gallery all round, reached by spiral staircases at two of the corners.

There was a huge leather-topped desk in the centre of the room with a massive armchair, covered in the same leather, at one side. Lady Carruthers sat in it and reached forward to open the main drawer. She drew out a large brown envelope, placed it on the top of the leather and took out its contents.

There were about a dozen full-size X-rays, mostly of someone's abdomen. She switched on a powerful table lamp, and invited me across to look at them. I held them so that the light shone through them.

'What do you see here, Doctor?' she asked me.

I was obviously on trial. She was showing me a full set of barium X-rays – the first few of a 'swallow' and the rest of an enema.

'How did you get these?' I asked her. 'Shouldn't they be in a hospital department?'

'They are mine,' she said. 'I always have them with me just in case they are needed. What do you think?'

I thought she was pushing her privileges as a hostess miles too far, but decided not to say so.

'The swallow shows you have a small hiatus hernia. The enema shows that you have diverticular disease,' I said. 'Quite a lot of it. What more do you wish me to say? Do you have many problems with them?'

'Not at the moment, but as you are going to be my doctor, you had better know what you are dealing with – and so had I.'

'Well, if you can make an appointment at the surgery in the next few days, I'd be glad to discuss it with you. But I'm not going to treat an X-ray. I'll treat you when you have difficulties with them, but maybe half the guests here tonight would probably have X-ray appearances like this. Many people have small hernias, and most of us get diverticuli as we grow older. Most of the time they cause no symptoms. It's just that you have the X-rays to prove them and most other people don't.'

'Are you saying that I have COMMON complaints?' she asked, obviously shocked.

Oh my God, I thought, I've done it again.

'Yes,' I said. 'Probably the two commonest complaints in older people.'

'So I'm OLDER, too,' she barked.

Maybe I'm not so good at this social mixing, I thought. I'm just getting in deeper.

'Well, over forty,' I said, lamely.

'So how would you treat them?' she asked.

'The best way to treat a hiatus hernia is to keep to a normal weight,' I said.

'So I'm FAT, as well,' she roared.

Then she burst out laughing.

'It's all right, Doctor, I'm pulling your leg. It's been a delight meeting you. You've done me a big favour this evening.'

'A favour?'

'Yes. You managed to insult my brother-in-law. He and my sister are going off in high dudgeon tomorrow morning, and they have cancelled their plans to come and live here, thank God.'

'What, just because of me?' I said, astonished.

'Yes. It seems you weren't too sympathetic to Hector, her husband. He doesn't take kindly to being told to stop the tipple.'

Hector, I thought. Good name for him.

'I'm sorry if I offended them,' I said.

She waved her hand. 'I'm not. I can't stand them. Let's go back to the others.'

We returned to the rest of the company in good spirits, she hanging onto my arm as if we had known each other for years. She rescued Mairi and me from the minister and his wife, then rescued us from further information seekers. How she made it clear to the others that they shouldn't talk more medicine with me I don't know, but she did. We have been good friends ever since.

CHAPTER NINE
BATTLING WITH THE MIND

Our first summer in the practice was idyllic. We finally found a house in Collintrae that suited all our family needs, with a granny annexe that could quickly be converted into a surgery, waiting room and dispensary. The local joiners, electricians, plumbers and builders went to work to transform it. It was sad to leave the kindly nuns, who had fought with each other for the privilege of baby-sitting, but their cottage was always going to be a stop-gap until we established a new doctor's house at the centre of the practice.

The two nurses, Flora in Collintrae and Jane in Braehill, proved to be worth more than their weight in gold as we started to organise ourselves. Together, we settled into a routine. The Collintrae villagers woke up out of their Tuinal-fed daydreams, and the Braehill patients were happy that I used a stethoscope and prescribed the pill.

However, the change wasn't always to the good. Stopping the barbiturates may have jolted the patients back into reality, but that wasn't necessarily for the better. Unsurprisingly, after months and even years of drugged suppression, problems like depression and anxiety started to surface. I began to think that, after all, Dr Rose had good reasons to prescribe what he did for some people. Worse still, for a very small number of my Tuinal swallowers, stopping it provoked more severe psychiatric symptoms.

Dealing with this upsurge of mental illness was a particular problem for me. Throughout my training and in my hospital jobs I had found it more difficult to deal with mental problems (now, it is politically correct to call them psychiatric illnesses) than with any other branch of medicine. Doctors are like this: we can't help it. There are some medical specialties with which we feel most comfortable, but most of us have an Achilles heel – a particular subject that we know we don't 'do well'. I have always been very happy with general medicine, with surgical emergencies, with accidents, with children's illnesses, with pregnancies and with the elderly. I am not over-keen on gynaecology, and am definitely at my poorest with psychiatry. I know that I have shied away from the subject when possible, passing on the management of mental problems to other doctors as quickly as possible.

To explain this, I have to go back to my earliest student days. When I left school, I spent the summer before going to medical school as a nurse in the geriatric ward of what was then called, without embarrassment, a 'mental hospital'. A collection of large Victorian buildings in the country, where the patients could be hidden away from public gaze, it housed hundreds of men and women who had been literally forgotten. There was no pretence at treatment – there was nothing to be done for them. Pills such as barbiturates (like Tuinal, but in much higher doses) were given to keep them quiet and biddable. Most lived in a state halfway between consciousness and sleep. They did not talk to each other, far less the nurses, who were more like warders than health professionals. These sad individuals were considered 'burnt-out' hopeless cases, who sat and stared, waiting only for their meals and bedtimes, when oblivion could, thankfully, overtake them.

A few younger in-patients with severe depression

(most of them had failed in suicide attempts) were given electroconvulsive therapy (ECT): I had the privilege of watching them convulse on a table, and of caring for them when the inevitable confusion ensued. Worse, a treatment in vogue then was insulin coma therapy, in which injections of insulin were given to deplete the brain of glucose. That made them unconscious, and they were brought round after a determined interval (how it was determined I still don't know) by an injection of glucose. Witnessing that scared me: some of the patients looked, during their coma period, as if they were dead, and I was always extremely relieved when they woke up again. They, too, faced the next few hours in a state of confusion. After a few hours they were back in the day ward, and it was difficult to say whether or not the treatment had helped raise their mood. One result was certain: none of the patients who were given the ECT or insulin treatment liked it or gave consent to it with a full understanding of its possible consequences. Any patient I was asked to accompany to the ECT or insulin rooms was always frightened and unhappy beforehand.

Worst of all was the 'square'. This was a yard in the centre of the hospital with a bare earth floor surrounded on two sides by the hospital walls, and on the other two by brick walls at least fifteen feet high. From here, patients could only see a small square of sky and quite a few of them in the yard spent a lot of time looking at it. It was like the exercise yards in poorer American B movies, where the unjustly imprisoned hero is under threat from the psychotic criminals, and often the psychotic warders, too.

Every day the patients who needed to be kept under lock and key were sent out into this yard for 'recreation'. Most of them just sat on the benches around the walls, waiting to be called in again for their meals and for bedtime. A few disturbed souls stood and shouted at the walls for hours on end. A small group were specially supervised in one corner. They had on thick canvas one-piece 'suits', with no pockets and no opening at the front. To get out of them, say, to go to the toilet, they had to ask a nurse to untie the cords that ran down the middle of their backs. Occasionally, there would be some minor altercation between two patients: they were immediately set upon by the duty nurses and taken into the wards, from where they might well be removed to one of the padded cells.

These were small rooms, just the shape and size of a prison cell, the walls, ceilings and floors of which were lined with a firm rubber. There were no windows and no furniture, so that the occupant could not harm himself.

He was placed there naked, so that he could not choke himself on his clothing, and locked in. Outside the door was a dial showing temperature levels. Turn the dial clockwise, and you could turn the cell into a virtual oven. The idea was to make the person inside so hot that they would be bound to calm down. The hospital had a dozen of these cells, most of them in regular use throughout my first summer there.

The ward I worked in stood by itself, in the grounds. Most mornings, just before seven, I cycled up to the door, past the main buildings, past the market garden and the hospital cricket field. It housed around eighty old men, many of whom had lived in the hospital all their adult lives, and who were now considered to be too old and too institutionalised to be a threat to anyone, including themselves. My first task every morning was to wake them up, take them to the toilets, wash them, dress them, sit them in their favourite seats, then make their beds. It gave me a real respect for the job of nursing, though not perhaps for particular nurses.

The atmosphere in that house – it was more of a community of old men living together than a hospital – is hard to believe now, looking back from the viewpoint of the liberated twenty-first century. The only doctor they ever saw was an eccentric Scot, Dr Haig, whom I judged to be near retiring age. Twice a week he would arrive at eleven o'clock, have a cup of tea, then do 'his round'. The old men were frightened of him: they sat up to attention when he spoke to them. All he ever asked them about was the state of their bowels. He never listened to their answers, but he ordered enemas for them, regardless. We dreaded his round, because we had to follow his orders. That meant taking the men to the sluice room, asking them to lie on a table there, and administering the soap and water mixture. As the junior, I was delegated to help the staff nurse with the task. The patients hated it, the nurses hated it, and I hated it. I couldn't imagine why we had to do it, because none of the men needed the treatment, as far as I could see. While I was performing this unnecessary, demeaning and brutalising function for them, I could see Dr Haig through the window, walking around the perimeter of the cricket ground, hands clasped behind his back, muttering to himself. He must have walked for an hour in this way after each visit to us.

As for the nurses, many of the older staff had come into the profession not because they wanted to nurse, but because it had been the only secure job open to them in the depression years of the Thirties. They had little sense of vocation: they looked on what they did as a job, and if they could relieve its boredom by finding some amusement in it, so much the better. Unfortunately, the amusement was always at the expense of their unhappy patients.

So every patient had a nickname. Mr Spencer, who believed he was the King of Mars (he really did) was called Donkey because at times he spoke in Martian, largely a very loud language that sounded like braying. Some nurses amused themselves by calling him 'Your Majesty'. That upset him, because he was on Earth incognito, and didn't want his real identity to reach the penny press. If it did, the Venusian king would send his hordes to 'see him off'.

Mr Harper, who predicted every day that the end of the world was coming tomorrow, was called the Doomster. On the famous day of the house's outing to Skegness, Mr Harper managed to wander away unseen from the rest of us, sitting docilely on the sands. We found him half an hour later haranguing the Butlin's holiday campers about their waste of their last few hours on earth in tomfoolery and frippery. What happened then still makes me ashamed to this day.

The two nurses in charge ran up to him, grabbed him by the arms, twisted them behind his back and frog-marched him along the prom towards our little forlorn group sitting on the sands. They shouted at him that this was the last time he would be allowed on a trip, but his mind was on other things. All the time he was being manhandled, he was shouting to the crowds walking by that the world was about to end and that they should save themselves. They stood still, taking in this scene of a poor deluded man being shoved around by two burly nurses and making no move to help. They tittered or laughed out loud at the spectacle that would make for light conversation later around the bars or in the chalets, but none complained that our behaviour was unaccept-able. I write 'our' because I was complicit in the scene. As a boy of eighteen I was very much the junior, and had no say in how Mr Harper was to be treated but I still feel that I should have spoken up.

My favourite patient was Mr Evans. The staff called him Penguin, because he had inherited a mixture of handicaps. Today these would have been lumped togeth-er in a 'syndrome' and his genetic problem would have been identified. Then he was just labelled with the main title of 'mentally handicapped', and the subtitle of 'near-imbecile'. Mr Evans had been in the hospital since he was thirteen years old – committed there because, walking in Lincoln High Street, he had stroked the hair of a young girl passing by.

For this heinous offence, he had been detained at His Majesty's pleasure – His Majesty at the time being Edward the Seventh. Since then George the Fifth, Edward the Eighth (briefly), George the Sixth and Elizabeth the Second all seemed to have gained pleasure from Mr Evans, because they kept him in the hospital for the next fifty years. He had not been beyond its doors, except for that annual outing to Skegness, in all that time.

Why was he called Penguin? Mr Evans was four feet six inches tall, and his build was not in proportion. His legs were much shorter than normal for the length of his torso, and he was unable to move them apart from his hips. He had to walk with a strange waddling shuffle, his knees clamped together, his feet turned outwards, so that they were set at more than a right angle. He bobbed from side to side as he walked, so that the description of Penguin fitted him exactly. His face, too, was bird-like, with a sharp beak-like narrow nose, virtually no chin and large protruding eyes. He was bald – I hesitate to add like a coot – another similarity that added emphasis to his nickname.

Why was he my favourite? Because despite his diagnosis of near-imbecile, made so many years ago, Mr Evans had become well read. In his early years he had been assigned to clean the hospital library, a room frequented by staff and doctors, but rarely by the patients, for whom it had been originally intended. Forty years on, having taught himself to read, he would speak quietly to people he could trust about all the wonders that he had read about in his days in the library. He was a gentle and kindly person, and would never have harmed anyone.

On some days I would be on the evening shift, arriving at two in the afternoon and leaving at ten. My job then was to make sure my charges were fed properly, toileted, showered and helped to bed. The evening medicine round also sticks in my memory. To make sure everyone slept well and in their own beds (men shut away from women for years had an understandable urge to share a bed – a habit that was illegal at the time), they were given a disgusting liquid medicine called paraldehyde.

At nine o'clock, the men formed a queue in the downstairs sitting room to receive it. The charge nurse, that is the head nurse, a male equivalent of a ward sister in a general hospital, stood beside a large table on which there was a huge brown glass bottle and two trays of small medicine glasses. Each man in turn would walk up to the nurse, be handed a glass that had been filled from the bottle, and would bolt down the contents. The glass would be replaced on the tray and the next man would be served with the next dose. There was a sink nearby, and it was my job to rinse out the glasses and replace them on the trays. Some of the glasses had red paint on them. These were to be used by the patients who had tuberculosis, and had to be rinsed in a different sink. The 'TB patients', as they were called by everyone, were segregated at mealtimes, too, eating in a small separate dining room, with red-painted crockery and cutlery. They slept on a verandah, since the hospital still had not understood that fresh air was no real cure for their illness. Even in the summer they were cold at night. I often wondered how they survived the winters.

Almost everyone on the ward was given the vile tasting paraldehyde, so that fifteen minutes after their doses, they were all asleep, snoring and grunting their way through the night. They called it their paralyser, and that's truly what it was. Years later, I realised that it was virtually an anaesthetic, and that their sleep was closer to coma than to normal sleep. The one person to be excused a paralyser was Mr Evans. Years before he had developed a severe reaction to the mixture and had almost died. It was decided that he was harmless and that it wouldn't be a problem if he didn't take it. He was

141

probably the only man in the whole place whose brain was still receptive to the normal rhythms of sleep and wakefulness.

Which was why I often sat beside him for the last quarter of an hour of my evening shift, when my routine work was done and I was waiting to cycle home. He was better company than the other nurses, whose main topics of conversation were women, football or the latest joke about some poor patient's aberrant behaviour. I asked him one evening if he didn't resent having been kept in this place for so many years, when he obviously was normal mentally.

'Look at me, Nurse,' he replied. He always called me nurse because, he said, I was the only one of the staff who called him by his proper name. If I was good enough to call him Mr Evans, he would give me my proper title, too.

'How would I have done out in the world looking like this?' he continued. 'I'd be in a freak show. The hospital has fed and clothed me and given me a bed. I've long since given up wanting respect and if they want to make fun of me, I can't complain. I've got my books and, now I'm old, that's all I need.' I marvelled at his acceptance of his unfair lot in life.

Around a week after this short conversation with

him, we had a new arrival in the house. Richard Brown was eighty years old. At the age of nineteen he had been sent to Broadmoor for the murder of a man in a pub who hadn't agreed with his political opinions. He had escaped the noose because at his trial it became clear that he was 'dangerously insane'. I know this now because I've researched the newspaper clippings of the time but we, the staff on the ward, were kept in the dark about his past. As far as we knew, Mr Brown had been transferred to us from another hospital because we had the room to take him, and he was now so old that he was no longer a problem. All he needed was routine nursing care.

Mr Brown arrived seated in an ambulance car with his small brown case in the company of two male nurses, which on reflection afterwards was unusual. Most of our 'transfers' came by public transport, usually a train, with a single attendant. He looked very fit for his age, clean-shaven, neat, well muscled, despite his advancing years. His light-blue eyes had a piercing quality, as if they looked right through you. My immediate thought was that it might be difficult to persuade him to swallow his paralyser, and my second was that, if he did, it might not work.

As I showed him his bed in the upstairs dormitory, I

tried to make light conversation with him, but he kept quiet, holding his head down, as if staring at some detail of the polished wooden floor. He clearly didn't wish to talk to me, and that was his affair. He put his few things in his locker, and followed me downstairs to meet the other men in the day room. I remember thinking that he had so little to show for his long life.

The charge nurse allocated every able-bodied man to a small job. Today it would be called occupational therapy: then, it was just an easy way for the nurses to avoid having to do the dirty jobs. On his second day there, Mr Brown was asked to help Mr Evans brush the dormitory floors. Mr Evans was happy to have him: at least this man hadn't yet heard of his nickname, and wouldn't laugh at him. I watched them go up the stairs together, and returned to my task, with the staff nurse, of making the beds in the sick room on the ground floor immediately underneath them.

We heard the bump about ten minutes later. It was as if something heavy had fallen over in the room above. Then silence. The staff nurse and I looked at each other, then dropped what we were doing and ran upstairs. Brown was standing looking out of the window, as if nothing had happened. Mr Evans was lying on the floor, a large brush beside him, the working end of it covered in red. It had obviously been swung with some force directly at his left temple, from where the red had stopped oozing. The fact that it had stopped wasn't good. The staff nurse bent over him, looked at me, and shook his head. For a second or two I wanted to rage and shout at Brown, but the feeling passed. He was in many ways as much a victim as my friend. He needed treatment, not punishment, and there was no treatment for him.

Naturally, the hospital held an internal inquiry. Oddly, my staff nurse colleague was called to it, but I wasn't. The superintendent ruled that as I was only temporary staff and 'only a boy', I couldn't add anything authoritative to its conclusions. However, he warned me not to speak about it outside the hospital, a subtle hint that if I did, I might not keep my job. Nor would it bode well for my medical school career. I wasn't well off. I really needed the extra cash – five whole pounds a week – to keep me going at medical school. So I didn't speak about it. In fact, this is the first time I have done so, fifty years later. I'm the only one left who knows about it.

Neither Mr Brown nor Mr Evans had any living relatives, or at least any who knew or cared about them. So the affair was dealt with quietly and efficiently. Mr Brown went back to Broadmoor, and Mr Evans was buried in the small plot near the hospital next to all the other forgotten human debris. He was seen into the ground by a vicar who had never met him, the men from the funeral company, the two gravediggers and myself. As far as I know, there was no inquest. Certainly there was no publicity about the case.

Even at eighteen years old, and still really a schoolboy, I knew that the way these men had been treated was wrong.

The next summer, after passing my anatomy and physiology courses, I had to make the decision on where I would work for my last long break before I started my time on the wards. After that there would be no summer vacations – we would be up at medical school all year round. I hesitated about going back to the 'house' but decided to give it another chance, partly because I knew the routine, and partly because, despite Mr Evans' death, I still enjoyed the work. And I sorely needed the money.

I was astonished at the change. In the main building, the rooms were brighter, and the patients happier. There were far fewer locked doors, and the walls of the corridors and wards were no longer painted in 'mental hospital' brown and cream. The wards and corridors were newly painted in bright colours and pictures, most painted by the patients themselves, hung on every wall.

The exercise yard was now a vegetable garden, with gangs of patients happily tending plants in the earth that had the previous year been a featureless expanse of unbroken clay. The padded cells had disappeared: the rubber had been stripped from them, and they were now used as study rooms or art studios.

What had happened? One big change was the introduction, earlier that year, of a single drug – Largactil, or chlorpromazine. It was the first drug to make a real difference to the quality of life of people with severe psychiatric illnesses, such as schizophrenia and personality disorder. The other was a change in staff. The old superintendent had retired, a younger man had been appointed, and he had brought a whole new breed of nurses into the hospital. He had also shaken up the nurse training school. I was hugely impressed by how a new broom could truly sweep clean.

There was another change. Dr Haig was no longer there. A younger doctor, a woman, now did the rounds. There were no more enemas. She was kind and compassionate, and she seemed to care about the patients' physical well-being.

But it wasn't the last I had seen of Dr Haig. One of the perks of the job was that the hospital had a cricket team. I was hopeless at cricket. My long sight meant that when I could see the ball it was too far away from me to hit it, and when it was within reach I had no idea where it was. In my seven years trying to play the game at secondary school I had never been able to hit a ball with a bat, except by accident. However, I was young and fit and could chase after a ball in the field, so I was asked to make up the numbers for matches. As they involved coach runs into the countryside to visit the other hospitals in the East Midlands, it was a welcome relief from the job. The team was a mixture of patients and staff, and we got on well on the journeys. The trips were classified as work, so I was even paid to go.

On one of these trips, to a hospital in Nottinghamshire, I was fielding in my allotted place near the boundary (my poor eyesight didn't let me field anywhere close to the bat) when I saw a familiar figure walking briskly towards me, around the perimeter line. It was Dr Haig. He was muttering to himself in his usual stance, bent forward, hands behind his back. As he passed close to me, for the first time I heard what he had been muttering.

'He needs an enema, he needs an enema,' he was repeating, over and over.

At the tea break, I mentioned to one of the team that I had seen Dr Haig, and asked why he had been transferred to the Nottinghamshire hospital.

'He's not a doctor here, he's a patient,' was the reply. The new medical staff in our hospital, in their review of the pharmacy stock, had wondered how it was that the hospital was top of the national league by far for orders for enema soap. Only then did they query Dr Haig's mental state and find that he was well into the middle stages of Alzheimer's disease. The transfer had been very discreet. Dr Haig was given his own room, and would wander round the wards ordering enemas, apparently under the delusion that he was a member of staff there. A short time later, I was told that he died, never realising that he was, in fact, a patient.

That story heartened me: the hospital service was human after all. The nicknames had gone, too. Patients were called by their proper titles. Mr Spencer and Mr Harper had both been given Largactil. It was hugely successful for the King of Mars. Mr Spencer still thought he was the ruler of the red planet, but he had lost his delusion of persecution by the King of Venus. He didn't mind any more that his secret was out. He confided in me that he realised now that Venus was an inhospitable planet that could never have supported life, and that all that stuff about its king must have just been in his imagination. He was much calmer, and the braying voice was down to normal volume. He was at peace with his self-imposed exile on Earth, and was regally and kindly disposed to all around him, including those who had made such a fool of him in the past.

Mr Harper's experience was less successful. He had responded exceptionally well to the drug, losing his sense of impending doom and becoming quite rational. He was so well, apparently, that under the relaxed laws of the new hospital regime, he was allowed out with a few fellow patients to walk to the local hostelry, a hundred yards from the hospital gates. However, on the way back he had crossed the road into the path of a fast-approaching car. Doom had in the end overtaken the unlucky Mr Harper, just as he had begun to think, for the first time in thirty years, that he might escape it.

I grew up in those two summers as a psychiatric nursing assistant. It was my experience there, more than all the psychiatric teaching at medical school, that had prepared me best for Collintrae and how to manage my little Tuinal-deprived band of men and women. But I wasn't truly prepared for my first real crisis, which came in the shape of Donald Gray.

CHAPTER TEN
DONALD GRAY

Today Donald Gray would be described as homeless, although he had a home that was perfectly accept-able to him. It had a magnificent view, a bountiful source of pure drinking water and plenty of other water in which to wash, on the few occasions he saw a need for it. It had adequate facilities for his sanitary needs and was perfectly insulated against the weather.

It was a cave.

The main road to Glasgow snakes its way north of Collintrae, between the shoreline to the west and the ancient raised beaches to the east. The first three miles are straight, built on the 'machair' land, the grassy flat area that lies between the coast and the richer, less salty farmland beyond. Then the road hits the Bennane Head, a granite hill over which it must pass to return to the machair again and the route that takes the traveller up the winding west coast, forty miles to Ayr and thirty more miles to Glasgow.

In the past, the Bennane was a real obstacle to travellers. It isolated Collintrae and the villages beyond it from the north, so that for centuries travellers to Stranraer and Ireland had to take the road miles inland. In the days before the road over the Bennane was built, in around 1890, the only way Collintrae folk could go north was either by boat or via Kilminnel and around the hills, a long detour in times when the only vehicles were horse-drawn.

So the Bennane was a place few people visited. Even in the twentieth century, people had not settled on the cliff top. The few farms there were set back from the edge, spreading into the hills beyond, and entry to them was from the inland road, not from the snake-like cliff pass. Yet for many centuries, people had lived in Bennane Head, in the caves below it, carved out of the rock by the pounding of the sea.

The nature of the caves meant that those who lived in them had to be special. So special, in fact, that they were often possessed of, for want of a more medical word, an unusual state of mind. For example, back in the fifteenth century, in the time of King James the Fourth, there was the Bean family. The head of the family was Sauney, who was reputed to have had several wives and many children, and to have eschewed all civilised behaviour. The mildest of this family's aberrations was that they wore no clothes, something that anyone who has sampled South Ayrshire's winters (or, for that matter, all four seasons) can hardly believe. Worse were their eating habits.

Sauney and his family were cannibals. People who were rash enough to take the cliff paths between Girvan and Collintrae had a habit of vanishing on the way. For a while, their friends and families thought that they had fallen off the treacherous cliff tracks by accident, until the 'accidents' became too frequent. When the militia eventually went to investigate, they found the naked Bean family well fed, with choice legs and arms hanging up, presumably an early form of the curing process we use for ham, in the recesses of the cave. The salt sea air was perfect as a preservative and, it was rumoured, added a certain piquancy to the meat.

Sauney was forced to watch his wife and children beheaded in Edinburgh before being exposed to the 'Maiden'. I won't describe it in detail as this is supposed to be a light-hearted look at Scottish life. It is enough to state that it had to do with a long, curved, razor-sharp blade and two heavy weights each attached to a leg. His quarters were then distributed to various townships and hung, rather appropriately, in gibbets for the citizens to ponder over.

Sauney's cave has not been lived in since that time, although today's visitors to it (they have to climb down a steep cliff path to get to it) are still finding small bones in the sand that forms its floor, or in crevices in its walls. Fragments of sheep bones, craftily broken to just the right shape and size, look remarkably like, say, the wrist bones of a long-dead ancestor, horribly slain by a Scottish monster. There is no scarcity of dead sheep around Collintrae, nor of locals who like keeping up the tradition of satisfying the romantic notions of their American cousins.

But Sauney isn't the main subject of this story. About a hundred yards south of his cave is another, with a high-vaulted, cathedral-like ceiling of pure granite. Its opening is just above the high-water mark, so that it never floods, and the sand and shingle floor gently slopes upwards fifty feet or more into the rock. About twenty feet in, there is a shelf on the north side of the cave, just wide enough for a man to sleep comfortably on, and high enough for the rats not to bother to visit. To the south edge of the cave opening, a fresh-water spring emerges from the shingle margin of the machair and the beach. It keeps running all year round, never drying up in the summer or freezing in the winter. Just in front of the cave is a large rock that hides its mouth from anyone on the sea beyond: it offers security and a natural break from the prevailing south-westerly winds.

It sounds like perfection for the sort of person who wants to get away from it all. Donald Gray was just such a man, the latest in a long line who had seen its perfection. The villagers would tell of a succession of recluses who had lived in the cave, going far back into their great-grandparents' time and probably long before then. The story went that, when one died, the next would always turn up within days, as if there were a grapevine for just this sort of loner.

Anyway, in my time in Collintrae, the cave occupant was Donald. With his long, straggly black hair and greying beard, his gaunt face, his ragged clothes put on in multiple layers in the winter, only a few of which he would shed in the summer, and his Wellington boots that were never taken off, even when sleeping, he cut a strange, but not particularly fearsome figure. The children of the village all knew him, and were never frightened of him or rude to him. Their parents had taught them to treat Donald with respect: they always said 'Good morning' to him as they passed by. He was as much part of the village community as they were. He had his nickname, as had all his predecessors. If you visit his cave mouth now, you will see on it a metal plaque to his memory, erected by the people of Collintrae, who held him in great affection. I prefer not to use it, however: he deserves a proper name in this book.

I can't say that Donald was a man of few words, because he wasn't. He was a man of no words at all. When I arrived in Collintrae he had been in the Bennane cave for thirty years, and no one had heard him speak a word in all that time. His routine was simple. Every day he rose at dawn and every evening, at dusk, he retired to his mattress on the shelf. They were long days in the summer, and very short ones in the winter. Throughout the year he tended a tiny vegetable garden on the machair beside the cave, grown from tubers, seeds and plants that were miraculously left just beside his cave mouth every spring. He foraged south to Collintrae on Tuesdays, and north to the small fishing village of Carletonfoot on Fridays. In each village, each week, he would find 'leavings' in the top of the bins. They were small offerings of wholesome food that the villagers had left specially for him, well wrapped in brown paper, so that he could carry them home to his cave.

Donald would never beg, or ask anyone for a favour, but he knew which dustbins were plentiful and which weren't. He never thanked anyone, but he would offer a gruff smile from time to time to those he knew had helped him.

That smile was a real effort for him. Donald had once had a promising career ahead of him somewhere in the city, but a devastating illness had deprived him of his desire to communicate any further with the rest of his kind. He was great with seagulls, with seals, with otters and even rats, but not with humans. I suspected that he had schizophrenia, but he had never been near a doctor in his adult life, having suddenly walked out of his parents' home, never to see them again, at the age of twenty. So I never knew why he had turned his back on the rest of us.

One of my responsibilities was to look after patients from the practice who were in the cottage hospital in Girvan. This took me almost every day on the road that passed only a few yards from the front of the cave. Often he would be sitting on a rock with his back to the road, looking due west, out to sea. It wasn't a bad occupation. In front of him were the rocks of the shore.

Beyond them were eleven miles of grey-blue sea with gannets and gulls wheeling high above it. Interrupting the skyline was the great rock of Ailsa Craig, the remnant of a volcano that was once higher than Everest. Twenty miles beyond Ailsa Craig the horizon was shaped by the long low hills of Kintyre, and to the north the majestic peaks of Arran. On a clear day Rathlin Island stood out in the south-west, marking the start of Ireland. I imagine he never grew tired of that view.

I stopped one day, to see if I could light a spark of interest in him. I clambered over the grassy hummocks, walked over a few yards of shingle, and sat down on a rock about ten feet away from him, facing the sea, not looking directly at him.

'Morning, Mr Gray. Nice view,' I said. I wasn't sure, but I thought I heard a very mild grunt. He didn't move his head or give any other indication that he knew I was there. 'I know you don't want to talk, and probably don't want me near you, but just in case you ever need me, I'm Dr Smith. You may know my car. I pass most days around this time.'

I thought I heard another grunt. I didn't want to press myself on him, so I stood up and left. He didn't turn round.

Over the next few months, I made a point of

stopping whenever I saw him walking along the road-side. I would wind down the window, smile and say hello, say a little about the weather and that I hoped he was well. I didn't intend to invade his private spot again, on the rock just above the high-water mark. But he never answered, though he did look at me for a second or two before resuming his trudge to or from his cave.

I eventually did intrude on his space around a year after we had first met on the shore. It was a beautiful June morning, the sea flat calm after a fairly severe storm the evening before. It had been one of those storms that the local farmers loved, because it tossed on the shore many tons of seaweed that they could harvest for fertilising their potato fields. Ayrshire tatties are famous for their taste, and just the right amount of sea-weed in the ground is one of the reasons for it. The shore-line just north of Collintrae is a good harvesting ground, flat and firm so that the tractors can be driven from the road right down to the beach. It is easy pick-ings, and gratefully received as one of the perks of living near the sea.

That morning, though, it wasn't just seaweed that had landed on the beach. I was first alerted by a phone call, at around eight o'clock.

'Is that the Admiralty Officer for the Collintrae

region?' said the mature male voice on the other end.

'I'm sorry, you must have the wrong number,' I replied, then replaced the receiver.

The phone rang again, seconds later. 'Excuse me, but you are the Collintrae doctor, aren't you?' It was the same voice.

'Yes, I am,' I said, mystified.

'Then you are the Admiralty Officer. This is the South Ayrshire police, Sergeant Duff speaking. We have a body you need to examine for us. It's on the beach just below the Bennane Head. Must have been washed up by last night's storm.'

'Why me?' I asked. 'Don't you have an on-call pathologist?'

'That's you,' said Sergeant Duff. 'As I said, you are the Admiralty Officer – it's part of the local GP job. Any body on a beach and you have to make the first examination. Only when you have certified death can we move the body. I don't think you'll find it difficult, Doctor.'

I thanked him for the call and drove the three miles to the Bennane, ruminating as I did that the job was throwing up surprises. There had been no Admiralty Officers in Birmingham. When I got there, I found that Sergeant Duff was right: it certainly wasn't difficult to certify death.

There were two police cars on the machair between the road and the sea, and a large black unmarked van ominously parked beside them. Three policemen were standing by, obviously waiting for me. James Brodie, one of the local farmers, was sitting on the machair grass, beside his tractor. The trailer behind it was half-full of seaweed. He had obviously been having a good morning, until he had caught sight of the object of our enquiries. Only twenty yards away sat Donald on his stone, staring, as he always did when he sat there, steadfastly out to sea.

The senior policeman introduced himself as Sergeant Duff. Mr Brodie had found the body as he was shifting a particularly bulky pile of seaweed from the shingle. As he had turned over the edge of it with his 'graip' (the Ayrshire word for a large fork), he had found two clear blue eyes looking up at him. Not surprisingly, he had been sick on the spot. For the eyes were the only flesh remaining on the face. The rest of the skin had been eaten away to the bone, so that the eyes were staring out of lidless sockets in a clean-picked skull. The only flesh to be seen on the head was over the back of the scalp and around the ears.

By the time I arrived, the policemen had cleared all the seaweed from the body, which was now lying face up, arms stretched out along the sides, one leg lying with an ankle crossed over the other. If it hadn't been for the lack of a face he might have been having a quiet siesta on the beach.

Beside one shoulder was a neat little pile of steaming half-digested breakfast, belonging to one of the policemen. Its producer was leaning against a rock a few yards away, apparently ridding himself of the rest of his morning coffee and toast. Another policeman, stronger of stomach, was busy taking photographs of the scene from different angles. Beautiful beach notwithstanding, these snaps weren't going into a family album.

I turned to Sergeant Duff. 'Well, he's dead,' I said, a little unnecessarily, I admit. 'What do we do with the body? We obviously have to take it somewhere for examination, and I doubt if the hospital mortuary would be happy to take him.'

'We'll put him in the south cemetery house in Girvan. We can do the post-mortem there,' he said.

'How do you mean "we"?' I asked him. 'Can't we get a man from Ayr?'

'It's up to you, Doc,' Sergeant Duff replied. 'The Procurator Fiscal only wants an external examination for the moment, but we may have to take a piece of lung.'

I blanched. I had had the usual student experience of post-mortem examinations, but they weren't my strong point. However, I couldn't let myself down in front of the men in blue. I bent over the body to make sure I hadn't missed any vital clue before he was moved. There were small black sea-lice jumping all over him, desperate to get back into the safety of the waves. There was seaweed in every fold of his heavy grey tweed overcoat. A red jellyfish had become entangled in its belt, so that there were strands of stinging tentacles wrapped round his waist. The backs of his hands, which were tightly clenched, were as bony as his face. The rest of him was covered with the coat and thick tweed trousers. I was astonished by how well his clothing had survived the sea and the creatures that lived in it. Obviously it wasn't nearly as much to their taste as his skin and flesh.

I wondered about his eyes, too. Why had they been spared, when they would have been the first meal for any crow that came upon a body left on land?

I stood up and turned to go, and as I did so, caught sight of Donald, sitting there, motionless as ever. I made my way clumsily over the twenty yards of slippery boulders and seaweed towards him and stood beside him, looking, as he was, out to sea.

'Morning, Mr Gray,' I said, quietly. 'You all right?'

I thought I heard one of his quiet grunts. I looked at his face: it carried his usual deadpan expression. If he had been affected by the body lying in his little piece of the world, he didn't show it.

'If you need me, let me know,' I said, and turned away, up to the machair and the road.

Sergeant Duff organised for me to meet him and two of his officers at six o'clock that evening, after dark, in the cemetery, where we would conduct our Fiscal's examination. I got on with my daily rounds and surgeries, then, at around five, I took out my books. I was the new boy on the block, and I had to perform. As a Birmingham student, my bible on bodies was Polson's *Essentials of Forensic Medicine* and as Polson had been very much a Birmingham man, there was not too much on bodies found in the sea. Happily, though, one of the books left by the late Dr Rose was the Glasgow tome by Glaister, and this had much more that was relevant to my current predicament.

So it was that at six that evening, I and four policemen, the extra one being the Fiscal's man, entered the gloomy shed in the old Girvan cemetery to perform the external examination. There was no electricity or heating, so we made do by the light and heat of three hurricane lamps as we began to divest the man of his clothes. Maybe I should have warned the policemen beforehand about post-mortem examinations of persons who have been dead a little while. But I didn't, which perhaps explains how, shortly after, I found myself in the shed alone, with four stalwart policemen outside, in various states of asphyxia. My mind went back to my first post-mortem attendance, as a third-year student. We were 'hands-on' students in Birmingham. That meant that our introduction into a subject was undertaken in the same way that young gannets learn to fly. They are just nudged off the edge of their cliff ledge by their parents. They free-fall a hundred feet or so, and just before they hit the water or rocks below, somehow they turn on their flying skills. From then on they can freewheel about the sky wherever they like. Presumably, millions of years of evolution have ensured that the 'slow-learning' gene for gannet flight has been lost on the way.

Medical school was like that. On our first day as students we didn't take part in the jollies and parties offered to the students from other faculties. Instead, we were introduced to the fearsome Ernie Jones, the Cadaver Man. Under his guidance we trooped up to the dissection room, were allocated our bodies and, on the sound of a bell, had to unwrap them and start to dissect the upper limb. We lost five young gannets on the rocks that first day, while the rest of us sailed on into the sky of our medical education.

By the time we were starting morbid pathology two years later, we were hardened to most sights and smells in the hospital wards and operating theatre. But I hadn't been prepared completely for my first full post-mortem.

My digs were on the south side of Birmingham in those days, and I travelled into the city centre, to the General Hospital, by bus along the busy Bristol Road. Unhappily for me, as it turned out, on the morning that I and the small group of students (the 'S's in the alphabet) were to start our pathology training, the road was busier than usual. The bus ground to a halt a mile from the city centre, stuck in a jam. I had to get off and run all the way to the General.

I arrived around ten minutes late, rushing into the mortuary hot, dishevelled and all apologies to the Professor. He was unusually cheery, I thought, all smiles. He didn't mind my being late at all, he said. I could have the last cadaver in the room. It was only then that I noticed that the rest of the students were standing by their tables, waiting to begin. On each table was a white sheet, under which rose the outline of a body. There were seven of us in all, and each of my six colleagues was standing beside a mound that looked of fairly normal size. Mine, white mound Number Seven, was different. It was huge. Underneath it was obviously a very fat person, with an enormous abdomen.

I grimaced, and realised why the chief had smiled. He had kept the biggest body for the last student to arrive, as a punishment for his laziness.

We were instructed for a few minutes on the rudiments of performing a post-mortem, then told to begin. I thought I caught a suppressed laugh or two as we removed our white sheets, and supposed that the Prof had let them in on his little wheeze. I didn't know the half of it.

A post-mortem examination begins by plunging a sharp knife into the upper chest, and drawing it down in one vertical slash towards the pelvis. We all did that. My memory of what happened after I did that to body Number Seven is very clear to this day. I can't really recall the faces of all the people in that room, or what exactly they said to me at the time. What has been imprinted on my olfactory memory for ever after is the smell.

My man hadn't been fat at all. He had been in a canal for three weeks and was full of gas. His body behaved almost exactly like one of those party balloons that you blow up and let fly around the room. Not that it flew round the room; it blew off the noxious agents that had been forming inside it during those weeks, in a concentrated stream. From being an enormous mound it quickly became a shrivelled, very thin, wizened little man, bathed in the most horrendous smell.

I staggered to the door, to find myself the only one in the room. Prof had warned the other students, and they had departed the instant before I had made my incision. They were out in the corridor, waiting for the fans to clean the atmosphere before they could start again. I was never, ever, late for pathology again.

The body from the beach wasn't quite as bad. The salt in the sea slows down the corrupting process, so that bodies taken from it are better preserved than those from industrial canals. Our mistake, however, had been to leave him at room temperature for around ten hours before examining him – by which time he had probably been out of the sea for fifteen hours. That's time enough to accelerate the rotting process.

Sergeant Duff managed to come back into the room to help me finish taking off the rest of the clothes. We took them off carefully, making sure we weren't stung by the remnants of the jellyfish. The dead man was wearing a coat, a suit, a thick white shirt, plain blue tie, expensive underwear, socks and high-quality brown boots that had survived their long immersion in the water exceptionally well. There was absolutely no mark of identification on any of them. Someone, presumably the man himself, had removed the makers' labels from all of them. There were no papers, wallets, handker-chiefs, combs, pocket knives – nothing by which we could identify him. The only objects found on him were collections of sharp stones in each coat and jacket pocket.

I propped up my copies of Glaister and Polson beside him, under the light of one of the hurricane lamps, and read, as I worked, the chapter on 'How to examine the body'. Sergeant Duff must have thought I was doing the equivalent of painting by numbers, but I needed to get this right. All the layers of clothing had preserved the rest of his body from the crabs and other creatures that had made such a good job of eating his face. He was a muscular man, with a moderate layer of fat on him. Much of the fat had turned into a substance called adipocere, a thick, greasy substance that Glaister calls suet-like. He also writes that it 'is inflammable and burns with a faint yellow flame: when distilled it yields a dense oily vapour'. He continues, 'it has a mouldy odour'.

Sergeant Duff and I already knew about the odour. We weren't going to test its inflammability, so we moved the sputtering hurricane lamp a little further away and continued with our morbid task. According to the two textbooks, this amount of adipocere meant that he had been in the sea for between one and two months. Apparently, he had never had a surgical operation or a wound – there were no marks or scars on his torso or limbs. I prized open his clenched fists, to find some strands of weed and pieces of stick still inside them. They were not from the sea, but perhaps from a river bank. His nails were scratched and edged with dirt that had survived the sea because the fingers had been tightly buried inside his fists.

I guessed from his skin, and the black body hairs going grey, that he was around fifty years old. I also guessed that he had committed suicide: many suicides want to obliterate themselves, to leave no trace of themselves in the world that they wish so much to leave. Removing all traces of identity is one aspect of this sad desire. The stones he had put there to weigh himself down but, perhaps, once in the water he had changed his mind. Were the twigs and grass in his hands the sign of a final vain fight for life?

As for the eyes, the explanation was there in

Glaister's pages, but it wasn't written by Glaister. It was a note in the margin, written by Dr Rose, just opposite the part about adipocere. He had obviously had a similar job in the past. It read: 'NB: the eyes are preserved in the sea – probably too slippery and solid for the crabs and the fish to get a hold.' I was grateful to Dr Rose and, as I haven't seen this noted elsewhere, I would like to call it 'Rose's sign'. You read it here first.

I had a last duty to do. The Fiscal had asked me to take a small sample of lung. It meant making an incision in the chest wall and removing a piece of the lung from underneath. The younger policemen, who had gingerly re-entered the room, decided at this point that the night air outside was better to breathe. Sergeant Duff, interested now, held the specimen bottle for me.

I had to perform a simple test. Salt water is denser than tap water. If you drown in the sea, a bit of your lung will sink in a glass of tap water. If you drown in a fresh-water river, it will float. This lung floated. I could there-fore give the Fiscal an assurance that, however the body got into the sea, it had arrived there from a river, around a month to two months before. I made the required report for a Scottish doctor reporting a cause of death – 'I swear on soul and conscience that I have examined this man and find that he has died of suicidal drowning. I do

171

not believe that any other person was involved in this death.' I thanked the police for their help and went home, for a large whisky and a long hot bath.

Next morning, I saw Donald again. He was still on his seat, looking out to sea. I said 'Good morning', he gave one of his little grunts, and we looked at the sea together for a few moments before I drove off.

I didn't think I would hear more about the body on the shore, but the dead man was identified a few weeks later. A real pathologist had performed a full Fiscal's autopsy. He confirmed that he had drowned in fresh water. Examination of scrapings from the soil under the fingernails and the plants in his hands had defined the area of entry into the water as near a bridge in the Upper Clyde. A man local to that area had been missing for a month, after finding his wife with someone else.

Believe it or not, it was the job of the police to launder the dead man's clothes and offer them to the not-so-grieving widow. After all, they were his possessions, and rightly belonged to his next of kin. Although they 'brushed up well', not surprisingly she refused them. So our local police force had disposed of them in a bin. A few days later, on my usual coastal drive to Girvan, I passed Donald, who was wearing a very fine pair of brown leather boots.

Though words were not for Donald Gray, I did once manage to get a dozen from him. Our second child, Alasdair, had arrived when Catriona was two years old. After that, to give Mairi a rest from time to time, I would take Catriona along with me in the car when going on short visits to patients I knew. They loved to see 'the wee lass' and made a fuss of her. She was a friendly girl, who smiled at everyone, including Donald when we stopped to greet him on the road or by the Bennane. Whenever I was accompanied by Catriona, a flicker of warmth appeared on Donald's face that I had never seen when I had greeted him alone.

From time to time, however, Catriona would have a recurrent illness that, thankfully, eventually passed. There was a period when she was around three years old when she had a long stay in bed and even a few days in hospital. The word got around the village that 'the Doctor's wee lassie wasn't well'. For a few days she was not in the car. When next I was driving past the Bennane, I saw Donald in the distance, waiting by the side of the road. As I drove up, he waved me down, the first time he had ever done so. I stopped beside him and leaned across the passenger seat to wind down the window next to him.

He stuck his weather-ravaged face through the space.

He looked anxious and was obviously trying to speak – it was almost as if he had forgotten how to do so. Then the words came out in a torrent.

'I hear the wee lassie's ill,' he said, almost in tears. 'It's no serious, is it? She'll be all right, won't she?'

Almost instantly, I could feel the tears flowing down my own cheeks. That this man could be so concerned about my daughter that he had spoken for the first time in many years moved me greatly. It took me some time to compose myself, before reassuring him and thanking him profusely for his concern.

From then on we managed to have the odd conversation. Donald died a few years later, still in his cave. Everyone from the villages around came to the funeral, and, the day after, the council bricked up the entrance to the cave so that no one could follow the old tradition. I thought then it was a shame, and still think so. I'm sure there is another Donald somewhere who could have filled his shoes.

Chapter Eleven
WILLIE'S HAIR

Willie had long hair. You'd think that wasn't so outrageous. But Willie lived in Collintrae.

The three Fs – fishing, farming and forestry – have sustained the men and women of Collintrae for a thousand years or more. It wasn't that the modern age had passed them by. They prized education and learning, but they didn't see the need to leave for the city when they had so much in and around Collintrae.

They were natural conservatives in those years before the rise of the Scottish Nationalists and the Scottish Parliament, though almost to a man they voted Labour, with a sprinkling of old Scottish Liberal. They followed their callings, father to son, mother to daughter, without a thought of seeking change.

Willie had followed his father and grandfather, and all the McIlwraiths before him, into the family boat. No rebel he. Yet he had long hair. It wasn't even a fashion of the time. Sure, there had been long-haired teenagers a generation before him, but at this stage the Beatles were wearing their hair in the Mod style, like an Eton crop. The long hair of the flower power people was yet to come. Only a cissy would have grown his hair as long as Willie did. But it would be a brave man who would call Willie a cissy. For a start he was a big guy. Years on the fishing boats had given him a formidable set of muscles and a weather-beaten look. So anyone tempted to snigger about his blond, curly, shoulder-length locks did it behind his back. Only his dad, Jim, the skipper, dared take him to task.

'That hair of yours needs a damn good clip. If you dinna get it done yerself, I'll get Alec McClung tae dae it,' Jim would say, though with tolerant affection, rather than anger.

Alec McClung was no fisherman. He was a shepherd, and the thought of his shearing clippers didn't go down well. There are no niceties about sheep shearing. Alec could shear a sheep every three minutes and keep it up for ten hours a day. Efficient, but not pretty. So Willie kept well away from him.

That decision saved his life, and I was a witness to it. I had taken on the mantle of local family doctor seriously. Now we call ourselves general practitioners, but I prefer the older name. It sits more comfortably with what I did – look after families. That meant learning a bit about what my patients did for a living, just as much as helping them when they were ill. So during my time in practice, I've tried my hand at sheep dipping and shearing, lopping trees and driving tractors.

I tried to think that it was just part of the job, then, when I eventually joined the herring boats for a night at the nets. I'm sick on the Arran ferry, and that's only an hour's trip on a ship a lot bigger than a fifty-foot inshore fishing boat. Herring congregate over the 'banks' about fifteen miles off the Collintrae shore. Look at it on the map, and you'll see that it's slap bang where the Atlantic rollers run into the mainland. There's no protection for three thousand miles: due west is northern Labrador, and nothing to stop the swell. I reckon the herring choose that spot out of spite. A few miles to the south and you are in the lee of the Antrim coast, and few miles to the north, there's the Mull of Kintyre, the hundred-mile long spit of land that runs down the west coast of Scotland, to protect you. But the herring banks? They're in the gap.

Herring are creatures of habit. They only appear for a few weeks a year, gathering in their millions at this forsaken spot to spawn. They don't choose the summer, either. Which is why I found myself going out to the fishing grounds on a bitter February night, sailing from the harbour on the good ship *Annabel* at around midnight. There were six of us on board: the five regular crew of four McIlwraiths and a McCrindle, and me. Jim settled himself into the wheelhouse and the others invited me to the fo'ard cabin. It was snug enough. Willie was brewing a cup of tea and Bud, his uncle, was frying a heap of bacon and eggs. I lasted around half a minute. The boat wasn't yet out of the harbour, and I was feeling sick. The smell of the bacon didn't help.

I staggered out on deck and decided to spend the rest of the trip there, watching the lights of home recede and the stars dance around with the pitching, tossing and yawing. Jim lashed me to the mast with strong rope, like Jason on the *Argo*, about to face the sirens of Scylla and Charybdis. He wasn't going to return to Collintrae minus the doctor.

We eventually reached the fishing grounds in about two hours of battling against what I thought must be a storm, but was cheerfully told was a force five – really only a breeze. Then the crew got to work. We were ring netting. That means that two boats work together. They start side by side, aiming to pay out a long strip of net. The anchor boat stays put, and the 'ringer' sails round in a huge circle, eventually returning to her partner. Each boat now has one end of the net, and it needs to be pulled in, hopefully full of herring. The fish swim at a certain depth below the surface, and the net is designed to work at just that depth.

What happens next is crucial. When the second boat backs alongside, its crew (apart from the man in the wheelhouse) jump across to the anchor boat with their end of the net, and they pull in the fish from that one boat.

On a calm night, that jump needs finesse: it isn't easy. When a two-metre swell is added into the equation, your timing and your jump have to be just right. There is only a second or two to make it with each wave, when the boat decks are at the same level. Willie, the youngest and nimblest, had gone on the *Carrick Rose*, our ringer, with Bud and Roddy McCrindle, a man of around thirty-five. They then had to make the jump back to the *Annabel*. I watched them, still tied as I was to the mast. The first to jump was Bud. The older man stood on the edge of the deck, waited till the two decks were level,

179

and stepped aboard the *Annabel*, as easily as stepping off a pavement. Roddy was a bit less sure of himself. He waited for a second wave to try the transfer. The boats rolled apart, then came together, the bumpers of old tyres hanging on the boat sides squashing together as they did so. He was a fraction late: the *Annabel*'s deck lurched away as he strode across, and he had to jump, just a little bit, to be safe. He landed safely and grinned back at Willie, who was waiting his turn.

The *Carrick Rose* and the *Annabel* swung apart again as a roller came between them. Willie was waiting for the trough, when they would swing back together. At the crucial moment he stepped off the *Rose*. Ocean swells aren't predictable. As he did so, a cross wind caught the side of the *Annabel*. I felt the jolt myself as the mast juddered against my spine. Instead of stepping onto the deck, Willie stepped straight into the water.

It happened so quickly that we were all stunned for a second. The boats rolled together, and Willie was under us. Aghast, I could only think he had been crushed between the hulls. The boats swung apart as the next wave came between us, and the water rose to meet the horrified faces of the men peering over the side. Both the boat and the sea around it were floodlit from powerful lights on the front of the wheelhouse, so we

'I felt the jolt myself, as the mast juddered against my
spine. Instead of stepping onto the deck, Willie stepped
straight into the water... The boats rolled together and
Willie was under us.'

could see almost as clearly as in daylight.

Five pairs of eyes desperately searched the churning surface of the water. Suddenly, just beside the hull of the *Annabel* appeared what looked like the head of a large floor mop. Bud grabbed it in his huge right hand. As the boats began to move together, he heaved with all his might. The mop came up in his hand like a cork from a bottle. Willie was underneath it, attached to it by his scalp. His feet were a fraction of an inch above the deck edge as the boats crashed together again. He hadn't even had long enough under water to take a breath. There wasn't a drop of ocean inside him, and his only complaint was that his scalp hurt.

He was taken to the cabin. I was unlashed from the mast and helped across the deck to tend to him. Naturally he was soaked to the skin, but a warm blanket and hot sweet tea soon revived him. His only physical injury was a sore head. We sailed back to Collintrae with a full catch of herring and a good story to tell. Strangely, the village found more to laugh about in my being lashed to the mast than in Willie's hair.

You would think that after such an experience I'd never set foot on a fishing boat again, but my duties as a doctor forced me back on the *Annabel* twice more in the following year.

Ailsa Craig sits twelve miles off the coast from Girvan and Collintrae. It's the remains of an ancient volcano, standing out of the water like the stub of a pencil, a thousand feet high and a mile across. The sea around it is deep and full of fish, so it supports hundreds of thousands of seabirds and a thriving colony of seals. In my time, it was also the home of the lighthouse keeper and his wife, and the small gang of men who from Monday to Friday hacked the granite from the cliffs to make curling stones.

Today, the keeper and his wife have gone, replaced by an automatic light. The granite gang has gone, too, replaced by a boat that arrives twice a year to blast the rock, collect it in huge lumps, and take it to the factory on the mainland to shape into the stones. The makeshift railway that carried the stones around the south face to the lighthouse and jetty on the east side has rusted almost away. When I see it now, I'm sad but realistic that it had to give way to modern practices. I still have vivid memories of my time there.

My first call came one winter evening at nine o'clock. Mairi and I had just finished a late dinner with friends. It was the keeper of the light. I didn't know him, as he was a Girvan patient, but his wife, Ethel, was listed as one of mine.

'Evening, Doc,' he said. 'Sorry to bother you, but Ethel has really bad stomach ache, and we need some advice. Could you help?'

We talked for several minutes about her pains, her sickness, her headache, and her bowels, until it became obvious that I couldn't make a diagnosis over the phone or rule out a serious condition needing surgery, such as appendicitis or a perforated ulcer. But how could anyone get out to Ailsa Craig, in the dark, with a storm approaching?

I asked the keeper about the Girvan lifeboat. It had already been called out to an emergency in the Irish Sea – and it didn't have a doctor on board. The only answer was for me to come in a fishing boat, if one was in the harbour.

My luck was out. There *was* one in the harbour – the *Annabel*. I phoned Jim, and he sleepily agreed to take me. He rounded up Willie and Bud, and prepared the boat for sailing. I took an anti-sickness pill, drove down to the harbour, and stepped gingerly and none too surely into the boat.

We took two hours to get to the Craig. There was no need to lash me to the mast – I stood alongside Jim in the wheelhouse all the way, staring at the light on the island to keep the nausea at bay. At twelve-thirty Willie, surefooted now, stepped off onto the jetty, then helped me ashore. We walked carefully over the slippery line of cobbles that led up to the house a few yards away, torches in hand. It was strangely quiet, the windows unlit. Willie rapped on the door. It took a minute or two for it to open.

The keeper was standing in his pyjamas, peering out at us.

'Oh Doctor, it's you,' he said. I had the fleeting feeling that this was probably the most unnecessary statement in the history of medicine. Who else could it have been but me?

'Do you mind if you don't come in?' he asked us. 'Ethel felt a lot better an hour ago. She passed a lot of wind, all of a sudden, and felt better. She's now sound asleep, and I don't want to waken her. If you come in she'll just wake up and lose the benefit of the sleep.'

Dear reader, what do you think I did? Did I turn away and simply go back to the boat, leaving the lady in peace but chuntering away about unreasonable patients under my breath? Or did I march in regardless and get my revenge, angry about the waste of time?

My first action was to count to ten, forwards, then backwards. I told myself that it was a reasonable call-out and also a reasonable request from the man. But I still had to go in – in the case of both appendicitis and a perforated ulcer, there's a time in which the pain goes away for a few hours, and the patient feels better. If the doctor misses that diagnosis, it's curtains for the patient. So I persuaded myself that I had to check. I explained this to the keeper, and walked into the cottage. Mrs Keeper was sound asleep, looking the picture of health. I woke her up and explained that I had come to check that she didn't need an emergency admission. I walked over to the sink and turned on the tap to wash and warm up my hands. The first lesson in clinical medicine was never to put a cold hand on a suspect abdomen. It not only upsets the patient, it also causes the stomach muscles to contract, which makes feeling for any abnormality much more difficult.

The colour of the water wasn't reassuring. It was light brown and smelled odd. I stared at it for a second or two, then asked how long it had been that colour, and if they had been drinking it. About a week, they said, and they had been boiling it before using it for cooking. They collected drinking water from a spring not far away, and used that for their tea.

Hands warmer, but not necessarily cleaner, I turned to examine my patient. Her abdomen was soft, though a little tender, and the bowel sounds were normal. If she were developing peritonitis the abdomen would be silent, and she would object fairly strongly to my putting more than the slightest pressure on it. She didn't.

I judged that all she needed was clean water to drink, and was able to give her a supply from the *Annabel*'s store. I took a sample from the offending tap for analysis, and asked the keeper to have a good look at the tank, on the hill above the house, when it was daylight. Before I reached the door, his wife was already sleeping.

By this time it was two in the morning. The wind had risen, and Willie and I walked back down the cobbles to the jetty, where the sea had covered the smooth granite flagstones with a film of weed and salt water. The cobbles of the road had offered some grip for the soles of my boots, but the surface of the jetty was like ice. Halfway down it my foot slipped. I would have been in the water if it hadn't been for young Willie's strength and fast reactions. In the dark, yards away from the lights of the boat, and with only torchlight to find me, I would have been impossible to find – especially as I have short hair. As it was I went tail upwards into a heap of seaweed. Willie caught me as I slid towards the edge, held me for a moment, then heaved me up. We walked the last few yards arm in arm to the safety of the *Annabel*. We took three hours to struggle back to Collintrae, against the wind and tides, and I fell into my bed at five-thirty.

The next day all was explained. In the surgery at nine sharp (in those days the doctor couldn't take a day off after a night up), I had a phone call from the keeper. The cover of the water tank had shifted, leaving a hole large enough for a rat to fall into it. Drinking eau de dead rat isn't consistent with a healthy gut even if it is boiled. The lighthouse supply vessel, thankfully, was arriving that day, and with the help of the crew he was going to put things right. In the meantime it was bringing a large supply of fresh water to tide them over. I looked at the sample on my desk, added a note about the rat to the form that was to accompany it, and put it into the box for the lab.

In the end, therefore, the visit was worth it, at least for the patient. It wasn't so profitable, however, for me. The slip on the jetty had driven seawater and weed, together with several sea creatures, under the surface of my oilskins onto my normal clothes underneath. Foolishly I hadn't changed on my way to the harbour. I had simply put on a spare set of Jim's oilskins over my best suit and shirt, with the sad result that my only tidy suit was ruined, as was the shirt. Talking to a colleague about it a few days later, he suggested I claim for a replacement from the Health Board. After all, wasn't a call out to the Craig in the middle of the night beyond the usual duties for a family doctor? Surely there was a fund that would supply some recompense?

I wrote to the Health Board in Kilmarnock. Two weeks later, I had a reply, with a postal order for ten shillings and sixpence. This was not a fee for the ruination of my suit. That, the letter stressed, was my responsibility. However, the Board could pay a fee for an out-of-practice emergency call. The rules were that the fee could not exceed ten shillings and sixpence, regardless of the distance or the time taken away from the practice. In fact, there was doubt that there was provision in my contract for me to leave my practice for such a time without employing a locum to cover me. They were looking into whether they should dock my pay for the appropriate time I was absent from Collintrae. I would hear from the Board later on this point. There's nothing like recognition for a hard day's work.

I had one more affair with *Annabel*. Three of the quarrymen who hacked out the curling stones on the Craig came from Collintrae. From Monday to Friday they lived in cabins on the island, working themselves to the limit. They were strong and tough, and at weekends they played hard, too. Pat O'Leary was in our famous village football team, a full-back feared by every forward who dared to pass him. Gordon Black and Michael Hagan were low-handicap golfers whose overdeveloped shoulder and back muscles helped them to hit their drives three hundred yards or more – though not always in the right direction.

The three had been great pals, as well as workmates, for more than ten years. The *Annabel* and the *Carrick Lass* were contracted, on alternate weeks, to take them and their provisions to and from the Craig on Monday mornings and Friday evenings throughout the year. They looked on it as the perfect job – with the boys during the week and a weekend with the wife and family. The absence during the week, they said, made their marriages better. I'm fairly sure their long-suffering wives agreed.

But no job is perfect. Which was why I found myself back on the *Annabel* one Wednesday afternoon, sailing for the Craig. The message we had from the lads' radio to the *Annabel* (there was no landline phone at the quarry) was that there had been an accident and that Michael's right leg was trapped under a granite slab. Pat had said that they had applied first aid and Michael seemed to be 'OK', but it looked as if he might lose his leg.

At first thought this seemed to be a helicopter case,

but there was no landing place near the quarry, and the winds and sea were making flying conditions very difficult, if not impossible. The Prestwick helicopter base would keep trying to get there, but could the *Annabel* make it, too, as the boat could get closer inshore and maybe arrive sooner?

Obviously we had to go. The *Annabel* had been fishing just offshore, so Jim took her into harbour, I climbed aboard (old clothes under the oilskins) and we set off. Luckily, tides and winds were on our side, and we made the crossing in less than an hour. Long-haired Willie grinned at me as he helped me lever myself from the boat to the rocks under the cliff, with tens of thousands of gannets whirling above and around us, like a blizzard of huge snowflakes.

It wasn't a time to stop and admire them. About fifty yards away were the two men huddled around Michael, who was lying calmly, waiting for us. I marvelled at his courage, as the rock that had rolled over his knee had obviously crushed it beyond repair. Gordon and Pat had made him comfortable, and one of them had saved his life by applying a tourniquet to the thigh just above the knee. There had been plenty of blood, but there was no bleeding now. The leg was hanging on by a thin flap of skin, and all I had to do was to cut it to ease him away, minus leg, onto a makeshift stretcher.

That was exactly the moment we heard the helicopter. We brought Michael down to the water's edge, as far as possible from the cliff above us, and watched as a man stepped out of the machine, along with a stretcher of his own.

It took only a minute or two for Michael to be carried away to hospital, leaving Willie and I to go home, and Pat and Gordon to carry on working. I was willing to take them back to Collintrae with us, but they wouldn't hear of it.

Six months later, Michael won the area amateur golf championship. I was there to watch his last round. He was brilliant. His drives were rifle-straight. He out-drove all his competitors by yards, and hit almost every fairway in 'regulation'. (Golfers know what that means.) His handicap had become 'plus' – four better than before his amputation.

Celebrating with him in the clubhouse, I congratulated him on his amazing recovery from such a calamity.

'It's my new leg,' he said. 'I've got a wee key at the side of the knee that locks the joint into place whenever I want to. It makes it rigid, so that it can't bend or sway. So just before I take my back swing, I lock it. That means I swing around a stiff right leg – I can swing the club down and into the ball in exactly the right path, every time.'

Obviously Michael couldn't go back to the Craig. The golfing success, though, opened up a new career for him. He became a golf assistant, and within a few years was club professional to a well-known course somewhere in Britain. I won't name it, because I don't know if he has told his members or competitors about his 'wee advantage'. And I don't know if it's legal to use it. Perhaps someone from the R & A Rules Commitee might know...

CHAPTER TWELVE
ACCIDENTS

The A77, the main road from Glasgow to Stranraer, is a hundred miles long. Twenty miles from its final destination – the ferry terminal for Ireland – it passes through Collintrae. To reach our little piece of rural heaven, drivers have had to battle through the towns and villages south of Ayr, none of which have, even now in the twenty-first century, been deemed worthy of bypass by the authorities. So that last fifty miles is a struggle on the best of days. When the weather is bad, or the traffic particularly heavy, there are hundreds of drivers hurtling towards Stranraer, desperate to catch their ferry bookings, unable to overtake on the narrow, wind-ing, two-lane road. Add a local tractorman going about his business, or a caravanner wanting to admire the scenery, and tempers rage. On days like this, misjudge your overtaking, and you end up at best in hospital. Impatience, tiredness, and narrow inadequate roads with blind bends and dips are a sure recipe for carnage.

As the Collintrae doctor I quickly became used to the call to accidents, sometimes more than one a day. On December 16th, 1966, I was called to two. I got to the first one, but I failed to attend the second. My memory isn't just hazy about the second, it's non-existent. I'd better explain.

As you drive south from Collintrae to Stranraer you first climb into the hills above Glen App. You enter the glen, which runs parallel to the coast, about two miles inland, through a narrow pass, with steep hillside rising up to the right, and just as steep a decline down to the left, through pine trees to the valley floor several hundred feet below. It was through this pass that MacAllan's bread van raced each morning at around six-thirty, with its load of freshly baked delicacies for the ferries.

On that December morning, it didn't make it. The driver was going too fast. A few yards past the summit of the pass men had been working on the road. They had closed off the right side of the road, so that large vehicles had to drive slowly and carefully past the obstruction, taking care not to catch the grassy verge, beyond which was the drop to the valley floor.

The baker's man knew that he had to go slow at that point, but he hadn't accounted for the black ice on the surface. The temperature was about three degrees below freezing and there had been rain the day before – just enough moisture to form a film of ice on the road, but not enough to notice in the dark before dawn.

As he edged carefully past the road-up sign, even at that speed the van slid enough to hit the grass with its front near-side wheel. The bus driver behind him saw the accident happen. The van had started to tip sideways as the verge gave way. As it did so, the driver's door opened, as if he wanted to jump out, but the tipping was too fast for him. Gravity slammed the door back onto him, and the roll of the van gathered momentum. The bus was close enough for the driver to see the headlights of the van spinning over and over, and to hear the smashing of the trees, as it careered through them.

I got the message about the crash from the dairyman who lived in the farmhouse at the bottom of the hill. Luckily, I was already dressed so I could leave home immediately. Warned by the policeman about the black ice, I gingerly made my way to the scene in my pride and joy, my blue and white Morris Oxford. Even going slowly I felt it slide on the various bends up to the pass.

I arrived at the scene before the ambulance, just after the fire brigade. Dawn was breaking: the December sun was making an effort to break through the swirls of grey mist. The firemen were at the edge of the road, shining a light down through the mess of broken trees at the wreck. We couldn't distinguish between broken branches and the remains of the bread van. As it had spun down into the valley, it had been ripped into shreds, so that we were looking down at thousands of pieces of splintered wood from the trees and the bodywork of the van. Scattered down the slope was an avalanche of hundreds of loaves of bread, rolls, cakes, flans and tarts. Below them, lying on the flat grass, was the cab of the van. And beside it was the motionless body of the driver, face down, limbs akimbo. We switched off the engines of the police car, the bus and the fire engine, to try to hear anything that might indicate that the driver was alive. All we could hear was the distant call of a screech owl.

One of us had to go down the slope, through the gap between the trees, over the jagged stumps and torn branches, to reach him. The firemen helped me into the full fireman's emergency gear of clothing and boots, tied me into a harness and let me down on a rope from a

197

winch on the back of the fire engine. I made slow progress over the slippery ground, over and sometimes through the mess of broken branches and stumps, down to the valley floor. I was sure that I would be examining a corpse: no one could have survived that fall. As I bent over him, the body turned over, and Frank Wilson looked up at me.

'Sorry, Doc,' he said, 'for getting you out at this time in the morning.'

Mr Wilson was one of my patients. His family lived in Kilminnel, and he had seen me once or twice for minor ailments. Everyone called him Lucky Frank because he had some years before won a few pounds on the football pools several weeks in succession. He had certainly been lucky that morning. All he had was a broken left ankle and a few bruises. He had immensely strong arms from years of driving large vans with no power steering. As he had first started tipping over, he had hung onto his steering wheel and braced his spine against the back of his seat. It was only when the cab hit the valley floor and the door burst open, throwing him out, that he had broken his ankle against its metal edge.

I signalled up to the men at the top, three hundred feet above, to let down a stretcher. By this time the ambulance had arrived, and one of the men came down with it. The three of us were hauled back up to the surface, Lucky Frank on the stretcher, and us beside it, to help steer it away from the wrecked trees.

This is where my account gets difficult. My next memory is waking up in a bed, staring at a bare light bulb. As I recall from forty years on, I tried to close my eyes, but couldn't. Somehow my eyelids weren't working. I was lying on my back. My head and face hurt, but I could move my limbs. A hand touched my right arm, and I turned to look at its owner. It was Mairi, sitting beside me, tears streaming down her face. She explained that I had been in an accident, and that I had been unconscious for twelve hours. She was pleased to have me back. She gave me the news that I was shortly to go to theatre to 'have my eyes fixed', then a nurse came into the room to wheel me away.

In the theatre another well-known face bent over me. I was lucky that Professor Jack Mustarde lived in Ayr at the time. He was the most famous plastic surgeon in the West of Scotland, who had trained with Archibald McIndoe in the Second World War, restoring the faces of burnt airmen. He and his registrar, Dr Ghosh, set about stitching what was left of my face together, under local anaesthetic. Jack cheerfully chatted to me throughout, explaining exactly what he and Dr Ghosh were doing, and what had happened to me the day before.

I'll draw a veil over my injuries. It's enough to state that they put over two hundred tiny stitches in my eyelids, forehead and cheeks. I still have the scars to this day but, as Jack said to me, they were designed to look like laughter lines and my 'face would grow into them'. He took photographs as he worked, and my 'before, during and after' pictures grace one of his textbooks of plastic surgery. I won't give its title, as they aren't for the squeamish or even for people with normal sensitivities.

He told me that I had been preparing to drive home from Glen App, when a police message had come through from the Bennane Head. A lorry had skidded off the road and hit a man, a Mr Gray, who had just stepped onto the machair from the beach. It was feared that he had serious leg injuries. Could the doctor please attend?

Perhaps I responded just a little too quickly for the conditions. But on my way down the steep and winding road from Glen App towards Collintrae, I turned a corner to face a lorry broadside across the road in front of me. It, too, had met the black ice. I'm told I braked, but that the Oxford swept serenely on, straight into the side of the lorry.

This was before seat belts. I sailed face first over my steering wheel through the windscreen (it was also the days before safety glass), over the bonnet and onto the road. Apparently, the lorry driver and his mate rushed to help me as I staggered to my feet, bleeding profusely from my lacerated face. 'We've got to get a doctor,' one of them said, to which I replied, 'I am the bloody doctor.'

My friends will vouch that I never swear. My father, a teacher, had dinned into me from an early age that people who swear must have no command of the English language. So I look upon my outburst as just being a statement of fact. I was certainly bloody and I was the doctor. Enough said. The ambulance carrying Frank from Glen App arrived a few moments later, and I joined him in the back. Apparently, he spent the hour and a half it took to get to Ayr helping the crewman look after me, riven with guilt for having brought me to this state of confusion and injury. I remember nothing of this, of course, because, as with any severe head injury, I have a permanent loss of memory for the time immediately before it and for many hours afterwards.

Donald Gray had been taken off by another ambulance, his left leg broken in three places.

Neither of us stayed long in hospital. It was close to Christmas, and it was decided that I could leave within a week, once the stitches were out and my concussion had recovered enough. It was a sobering time. I have a big head — a hat size of seven and three quarter inches. I used to take secret pride in the knowledge that I had an exceptionally large brain. My skull X-rays soon put paid to that. They showed that my unusual head circumference was nothing to do with my brain size. Instead, my skull was at least one and a half times as thick as normal skulls. I wasn't an egg-head but a bone-head — something that I'm sure my friends had suspected for years. On reflection, though, this wasn't a bad thing. The extra bone thickness meant that it was better able than most skulls to withstand knocks such as being hit by a hard object, viz. one windscreen, at about thirty miles an hour.

Donald Gray was out of hospital long before me. He had been put into a plaster of Paris bandage that stretched from one hip to his foot, so that he could not bend his hip, his knee or his ankle. He was meant to stay in this hard casing for several weeks, preferably in hospital where he could be looked after properly. As his official address was 'Number 1, Bennane Cave, Collintrae', the social services felt that he would not be returning to a home conducive to a good recovery so they had put him in a ward.

On the first night, however, he had heaved himself

out of his bed, wrapped a dressing gown around the nice new nightshirt so thoughtfully provided by the hospital and, while the nursing staff were attending to some other more needy person (it might even have been me), walked out of the back door of the hospital onto the street. As the hospital was next to the main road to the south, it wasn't long before a kindly lorry driver, ferry-bound, picked him up, nightshirt, plaster, hospital slippers and all, to deposit him by his cave. All the lorry drivers knew him. Like the villagers, they too left the odd brown paper parcel by the roadside, next to his cave, and they had all heard of his mishap.

As for me, the local Health Board found me a locum doctor, who had just retired from a busy practice in Kilmarnock, to take over my duties for the next month or so. Dr Jimmy Anderson turned out to be the silver lining to the cloud of my accident. He did a massive job for me in looking after the practice, and he decided at the end of his month to move to the district. He became my regular locum for the odd weekend and week away, and continued to do the job for my eventual successor until he was into his late eighties, becoming a very good friend.

As for Mr Gray, he kept on his hip plaster until the following May, around four months after its sell-by day was past. He steadfastly refused to go back to the hospital for its removal, and he waved away any attempts by myself or Jimmy to let us remove it. All through the rest of the winter and well into the spring, people who passed by the Bennane were regaled with the sight of Mr Gray waddling about with a huge white, then grey, then black plaster from hip to ankle. We marvelled at how fast he could move with it. Eventually, I sat down beside him and suggested that he might let me remove it. This was before we had started to talk. His little grunt gave me hope: I returned to my repaired Morris Oxford and brought out the plaster scissors and knife.

He kept staring out to sea as I removed the plaster. The leg underneath had healed perfectly. It was strong and healthy, with no sign of any deformity from the three breaks. We threw the plaster onto the fire that burned constantly at the mouth of his cave and held a silent cremation ceremony around it. Donald looked at me and grunted again. There was even a slight nod of the head that I took for a thank you.

Four years later, I was called one spring morning to the Bennane Head. This time a van had failed to take a bend at the summit of the hill. The driver of an approaching car had seen it plunge off the road, through the flimsy barrier, over the cliff edge to the sea two hundred feet below. I got there at the same time as Nurse Flora and the ambulance men, the same crew who had helped on that December morning.

The four of us stood at the broken barrier and looked over the cliff edge at the boiling sea below. I was experiencing déjà vu. There was the splintered wood with the bakery colours on it, the hundreds of loaves, rolls and cakes littered all the way down the cliff face and floating on the sea. The cab was by now deep in the water. We could see the driver's body lying face down, spread-eagled inches from the shoreline. He was yards away from the sunken cab, so we assumed that he had been thrown out before the cab had hit the sea.

This time we were sure we were dealing with a death. Flora and I were lowered down to inspect the body. As we approached, it turned over, and Lucky Frank looked up at me. 'Hi, Doc. It's me again. We have to stop meeting like this,' he said.

His only injury was a broken ankle, the other one this time. He told us that he had fallen out of the cab when it bounced against a rocky projection. As luck would have it, he had landed on the only hillock of spongy sea grass and moss. A few feet in any direction away from it were either rocks or sea. His ankle had broken, just as it had last time, when it caught against the door frame on the way out.

Lucky Frank, Flora and I were hauled up by the ambulance team. Frank and the men had a reunion at the top of the cliff, and they took him off to the hospital to sort out his ankle.

Even though he had wrecked two vans, the bakery didn't sack him. They did take him off driving duties, however. They promoted him to store manager, a job in which, as far as I know, he had no more disasters.

CHAPTER THIRTEEN
CHILDREN

To be appointed to a single-handed practice back in those days, doctors had to show evidence of experience in children's medicine – essentially that meant having worked for at least six months as a junior doctor in a children's hospital. I did my stint in the Birmingham Children's Hospital, the busiest children's hospital in Britain outside London. Learning from textbooks and ward rounds as students was all very well, but what we learned as housemen truly fitted us for our role in general practice.

For example, no textbooks list the condition of LSD-CHD. This was a favourite diagnosis of our consultant surgeon, Vincent Burns. He was a massive man with huge hands to match, yet he could use them on the tiniest of babies with unsurpassed skill. It was a privilege to work in theatre with him, but he was at his best for us housemen in the outpatients' department.

When I first saw him, in one of his clinics, scrawl LSDCHD across a small boy's notes I hadn't a clue what it meant. I was too shy to ask him outright. By the time the session was over, he had made the diagnosis three times, and three small boys went home happily with their mothers, safe in the knowledge that they had nothing to fear from his knife.

LSDCHD stood for 'Lady School Doctor's Cold Hands Disease'. It doesn't take much imagination to understand why. In those days, school doctors examined every five year old. The boys had to drop their trousers, and the doctors felt to make sure they had two testicles in the right place with no ruptures. One of the lady school doctors must have had poor circulation because, at the touch of her fingers, the boys' tiny scrota contracted and the testes disappeared like rockets up into their groins. Cold fingers have the added disadvantage of being less sensitive than warm ones, and the tiny testes responded so fast to their touch that the lady assumed that they had never reached their proper position. Children whose testicles had never descended had, of course, to have corrective surgery. Hence the constant flow of boys to Vincent Burns' clinic. Eventually, it is said, he sent the unfortunate doctor a note, plus a small hand warmer that people use when playing golf in cold weather. From then on, LSDCHD was extinct.

My main duty in the hospital was as house physician to Dr William Carter, who has been the biggest influence on how I practise medicine. He put kindness and consideration above all else, but was no slouch at diagnosis and, whenever it was possible, treatment. I write that with some sadness, because most of his patients were fatally ill. They either had lethal cancers, mainly leukaemias and brain tumours, or had inherited fatal illnesses that would cut short their lives before they could grow up.

I spent Christmas in the hospital, at the height of the Beatles mania. Four of us dressed up as the Famous Four, with wigs and dummy guitars and drums, and we travelled round the wards miming to their records. I was Ringo, totally without any sense of rhythm or talent, yet when we reached my ward I got a special cheer from my little bunch of brilliant kids.

One of the boys in particular stays fresh in my memory. Gregory was the last of three brothers. He was only eleven years old, and he, like the two before him, had a condition called Fanconi's syndrome. I looked after him during his final few weeks. He was well aware, from his experience with his brothers, that he had no hope. We have learned now, forty years later, that his disease is caused by a single mutation in a gene. Then, all we knew was that he had inherited a condition that stopped his bone marrow from making red blood cells, arrested his growth, gave him a squint and made his kidneys fail. I gave him numerous blood transfusions, then tried to make him comfortable as his kidneys finally gave up. There were no kidney dialysis machines for children then, nor were there transplants. Yet Gregory kept his sense of humour to the end. He had a super Christmas day, with presents from all the staff. We Beatles spent an extra ten minutes round his bed, and he was laughing just a little while before he fell asleep for good.

That day I made the decision not to continue with paediatrics. I knew that I couldn't face the endless stream of tragedy that I would have to deal with. I needed to find a branch of medicine that would offer happier endings, yet still let me work with children. General practice seemed to be the only one.

The face of one more child of that time is still very

clear to me. He was called Alfie Brownhill, and he was an eight-year-old imp. Usually a very energetic and well co-ordinated boy, in the two weeks before he had been sent to us he had started to stagger at times, and complained of headaches. At first his mother thought they were migraines, just like the ones she often had, but when they continued, she at last took him to his doctor, who immediately sent him to us. We were a brain tumour ward, and the doctor thought that this was the diagnosis.

At first we thought the same, but when Alfie himself suggested that the start of the headaches and his difficulty with balance might be linked to a recent fall in the local swimming pool changing room, we changed our minds. He was right. He had hit his head on a tile when falling, and it had cracked a bone in his temple. The sharp surface of the fracture had torn a blood vessel underneath, and blood oozing from it had formed a clot on the surface of his brain, the medical name for which is subdural haematoma. This had led to pressure on his brain, which had caused his symptoms. We were thrilled to find that clot, because it meant we could do something to cure his problems – something of a rarity on the ward. The surgery was successful, the clot was removed, and he became a normal little boy again.

Good as his story is, it isn't the reason I remember him. No, my sharpest memory of Alfie is of the day he was presented as a 'case study' to the rest of the hospital medical staff. Once a week all our teams of doctors, students and nurses met to hear presentations of unusual 'cases'. Alfie, having been both a medical and surgical patient, was going to be shown to us by the medical registrar, Jane Fulton, my senior by two years. She first said a few sentences about the investigation of headaches and balance problems, then asked my opposite number on the surgical ward, Manu Tailor, to show Alfie to the audience.

As Manu wheeled Alfie, in pyjamas, dressing gown and part-shaven head, onto the stage, Dr Fulton started her talk.

'This is case number 63-52,' she said. 'To summarise first. Three weeks ago, he hit his head against a tile floor and sustained a skull fracture and a subdural haematoma. I am going to demonstrate the physical signs and the intellectual deficit that he has incurred.'

'Oh, no, you are not,' came a small voice from the stage. 'I'm not a number. My name's Alfie Brownhill, and I know what intellectual deficit means.'

Alfie then looked round at Manu. 'Can you take me out of here?' he asked.

I keep Alfie's little speech in the front of my mind whenever I'm with children. They know and understand far more than we adults credit them with, and they have a very strongly developed sense of what is fair and what isn't. Knowing these children shaped how I looked after children in general practice, though they were unusual.

Much more commonplace were the infectious illnesses that still plagued children in the Sixties. Today's doctors hardly ever see them, but mumps and measles then claimed dozens of lives a year in Britain from the complications of brain infections, and we had our share of these tragic children. The most frightening of these childhood infections for families and doctors alike was meningitis.

Children struck down by meningitis could then, and can still, go from good health to death in one or two days if it is not diagnosed and treated quickly with a penicillin injection. My hospital experience of children who arrived too late made me swear to myself that I would never be without a penicillin injection in my bag, and that I would never give advice about a child to a parent over the phone.

It wasn't long before I was blessing that decision. From the start of my GP practice at Braehill, I tended to plan my routine visits on the other days of the week, so that on Sundays I had only emergencies to deal with.

The Stinchar Valley people proved to be very considerate, invariably calling me before ten in the morning so I could plan my day. I would enjoy seeing the odd patient on a Sunday morning, then relax over lunch, and perhaps wash the car in the afternoon. I couldn't stray far from the phone – as the only doctor on duty I was on call twenty-four hours a day. But there was plenty to occupy me at home – the fast-growing Catriona, the car to wash, and the river to watch for leaping salmon and the otters chasing them.

When I received two calls to children in Collintrae at around nine-thirty one warm Sunday morning, I was quite pleased to drive the thirteen miles to see them. The families that called me were only three doors apart, so I could walk easily from one house to the other. The two three-year-olds had identical sore throats. They played a lot together, were in the Tufty club together (it was a predecessor of the modern play groups), and one had obviously infected the other with the same germ. Apart from their throats, they were reasonably well, perhaps a little feverish and with aching limbs, but nothing more. I felt able to dispense from my emergency bag a penicillin suspension for each of them, and was confident that they would do well on rest and their mothers' care. I drove back home feeling that the visits had been worthwhile, and Mairi had a coffee waiting for me.

She disappeared out of the back door of the cottage while I was drinking my coffee. The phone rang. It was a farmer reporting that his wife had stomach pains, and asking for some advice over the phone. It didn't sound straightforward, and when I told him I would visit, I could hear the relief in his voice. I walked outside to find Mairi hosing down the car. It was still dripping wet and shining in the sun when I opened the door, explained where I was going and drove off. I left my long-suffering wife standing there with cloth and bucket in hand mouthing what I hoped, but wasn't sure, were pleasantries.

The farm was up in the hills above Kilminnel. Like all the hill farmers, the MacTaggarts bred beef cattle, sheep and a few pigs. The animals ranged free all summer over the moorland, and only came into the steading when the calves were going to market and the sheep were sheared and dipped. The house was built on one side of a large square courtyard, two sides being devoted to barns and sheds, and the fourth was open for access to the road.

I drove into the yard, shut the car door and walked

through the kitchen doorway into the farmhouse. It turned out that Mrs MacTaggart's stomach pains were due to a simple bladder infection which was easily treated.

Once I had arranged for some medicine for her, I turned to go, but was stopped by the phrase that causes the hearts of all doctors to sink.

'While you're here, Doctor,' said Mr MacTaggart, 'could you look at the wee lad? He seems to have a sore throat and is a bit off-colour.'

I didn't mind at all. I knew wee Sandy MacTaggart. He was always full of energy and had been to see me on several occasions for minor injuries from falling off farm machinery or from enraged animals that he had teased.

Sandy certainly wasn't himself. Aged four, he too was a Tufty club member, and had been playing with my two little Collintrae patients two days before. He was lying on the couch in the living room, eyelids drooping, tired and listless. He didn't admit to a headache, but he found it sore to swallow anything. Anyway, he wasn't hungry – a real change for him. I looked at his throat, saw that it was just the same as the other throats I had seen that morning, assumed he had the same germ, dished out yet another bottle of penicillin medicine and reassured his worried dad. He was bright enough to give me a wave as

I climbed into the car and reversed across the yard.

I was really pleased when I saw Mr MacTaggart waving enthusiastically, too. For a fleeting moment I thought that I must have pleased him a lot, until the world outside the car suddenly disappeared in a thick brown mist. My back wheels were spinning, but my car was moving no further backwards, and the mist was deepening by the second. I put the gear into neutral, stopped the engine and gingerly opened the door. I should have taken it even more carefully, as foul-smelling brown liquid dripped into the car and onto my trousers and sleeves. The back wheels were sunk up to the hub caps in a pile of what I first thought was manure. I later learned that the technical term for this material is slurry, and that I had reversed into the farm midden, where all the animal waste was piled up each year, eventually to be spread across the fields.

Mr MacTaggart was most kind. He brought out his tractor, attached a tow rope to my front axle (luckily, it had not got as far as the midden) and pulled my car out. He even offered to clean it for me, but it was getting close to lunchtime and I had clothing to change. I arrived home in a car that was a uniform khaki colour, except for the patch of windscreen that I had had to clean to see through.

My reception back at home wasn't quite as warm as I had hoped. My car, which Mairi had so thoughtfully cleaned only an hour before, was not only unrecognisable but smelled like a badly run sewage works. And my Sunday suit wasn't fit for a doghouse.

So it wasn't the best of atmospheres in the Smith household when we prepared, finally, to eat our Sunday lunch. I was just pulling my chair back to sit down when the phone rang.

'Dr Smith here, can I help you?' I said, hoping I didn't sound as grumpy as I felt.

'Henry McHarrie here,' said the man on the other end. I knew Henry well. He was the Collintrae plumber. Everyone called him Happy Henry because, no matter what adversities he faced in life, he always smiled and joked about them. Which was just as well, because he wasn't exactly the world's best plumber. After Happy Henry had called, there were times when cisterns overflowed, cold taps ran hot, WC flush levers worked upwards instead of downwards, and radiators leaked. But he was an enthusiast and what he lacked in exceptional plumbing skills he more than made up for by helping anyone in distress. He was also the goalie in the village football team. He was a much better goalie than a plumber, and that was enough to keep him popular among his customers.

He wasn't quite as cheerful, however, that day.

'I don't want you to come out, Doctor,' he explained. 'Me and the missus would just like a bit of advice about young Thomas.' Thomas was Henry's two-year-old pride and joy, a late son for the couple, born ten years after they thought they had completed their family of four.

'He hasn't been himself all morning,' Henry continued. 'He started by saying his throat was sore, and he's a bit hot and sweaty. Just now, he has been a bit sick, and he seems to be rambling a bit. I know you've been down to the neighbours this morning, and we wondered if Thomas might have the same as them. Is there anything we can do without you having to come out?'

That was kind of him, I thought: I could ask him to go next door. It sounded as if Thomas had the same 'bug' as the others. The neighbours would let him have a few doses from their medicine that would do until tomorrow. There wouldn't be any harm in that.

But then I fully took in what Henry had said. Thomas didn't just have a sore throat, he had been sick, and he was 'rambling'. None of the other children I had seen that day had had either of those symptoms.

'I'll come to see you right now,' I said, and put the phone down. Mairi looked at me.

'I'm afraid it can't wait,' I said, picking up the emergency bag and walking out of the door towards my still fragrant, slurry-coloured car.

I took fifteen minutes to get to the McHarrie house and a further minute to see that I was faced with meningitis. Young Thomas was lying on his back on the bed, his head arched backwards, his back curved upwards, so that only the back of his head and his heels were actually touching the bed. His spine was stiff and there was the beginning of a rash across his upper tummy. I pressed a glass against the rash: it didn't fade under the pressure. I had no doubt about the diagnosis. I was glad I hadn't waited to eat my lunch. Minutes mattered.

I gently told his parents what I was doing, and gave him an injection of penicillin. The emergency ambulance was there within minutes and he was away to the Ayrshire fever hospital in Irvine shortly afterwards.

I wasn't hopeful about young Thomas, but he recovered well, with no final damage to his brain as far as we could see. Today he is as big as his dad, whom he followed both into the goalposts and the plumbing business, and just as affable. Everyone calls him Happy Tam, and from time to time he offers to wash my car, then laughs like a drain. Which is appropriate, I suppose, for a plumber.

Chapter Fourteen
WHILE YOU'RE HERE, DOC

I'd like 'While you're here, Doc' on my tombstone. It's the phrase that doctors have nightmares about. The TV detective Columbo knows exactly how to use it. You surely know the series. Our raincoat-clad hero shambles to the door after a seemingly painless interview with the man we already know has committed the murder. He thinks he has got away with it. As Columbo puts his hand on the door handle, he turns, puts a finger to his forehead in puzzlement, looks at his quarry, and says, 'There's just one thing that's worrying me.'

That scene, slightly changed, is repeated time and again in a doctor's life. Except it's the patient who remembers, at the end of the consultation, the vital

221

thing that he or she really needs to know about. It's called in the trade 'the hand on knob' question.

In my early days, in Birmingham, the hand on knob question was almost invariably about contraception. The 'pill' had just been introduced, and couples were still shy about asking for it, or even talking about sex at all. It took a decade or more for people to lose their shyness about it, especially with a young male doctor like myself.

In the Stinchar Valley, however, my country patients were much more direct. With animals all round them, sex was just a matter of course. They could organise that for themselves without any help from me. No, their hand on knob questions were usually quite different.

The first time it happened was on a wild March night. I had been called by a farmer, Rab Jackson, because his wife had a bad cough, had chest pains and 'was a bit breathless'. She had been suffering like this for a few days, he said, but now he was worried because she hadn't been fit enough to make his evening meal, and was just lying on the sofa, 'wi' no enough puff tae get up'. Could he possibly be more concerned that his food wasn't on the table than that his wife was ill? Surely not.

The farm was about six miles from Collintrae, at the end of a winding country road, and it took me about fifteen minutes to get there. As I got out of the car I could see that men were flitting about in the byre – the cowshed – next to the house. One of the men called to me from the byre doorway. His back was to the light streaming out from the byre, so at first I didn't recognise him.

'Hey, Doc, seeing you're here, could you give us a hand?' It was Rab.

I walked over to him, to find that he and another man were in the middle of a maternity case. It wasn't human, of course, but a cow. The poor animal was standing with her back to me, rear legs wide apart, with a large wooden tripod contraption fixed up against her nether end. The tail had been tied up out of the way, and a thick rope was projecting out of her birth orifice. The near end of the rope was wrapped around a drum on a winch: the far end, I gathered, was tied around the presenting part, hopefully the front legs, of the unfortunate calf deep inside her.

I assumed that this was the bovine equivalent of a forceps delivery. The aim was to start the winch as soon as the cow's womb contractions came, so that the rope was pulled only along with the contractions. The tension in the rope was eased when the contractions stopped. Pulling at the wrong time could pull the uterus out with the calf, killing both. The men's problem was that with one man at the winch and the other leaning on the tripod, they needed a third at the cow's belly to feel for the contractions. I was a godsend – not only could I help them, I was surely used to feeling for contractions, though hardly of such a massive nature.

I stood beside the cow with a hand on its underbelly and listened to it bellow as another contraction started. There was no gas and air to ease the pain. I signalled the winchman to start up, and the rope became taut. It took another two contractions before suddenly the calf was born, falling three feet from the birth canal onto the concrete floor of the byre. The men didn't think this was a problem – and it wasn't. After a few minutes the calf shook himself and his mother bent round to lick him and start to eat the membranes.

I marvelled at the sight and, a few minutes later, marvelled again to see the calf stand up shakily and search for his mother's teats.

There was backslapping and grins all round.

'Good job well done,' roared Rab. 'Come in and have a wee half to celebrate,' he added.

'But I'm here anyway to see your wife,' I said, now a bit guilty that the calf seemed to have taken precedence over the human patient.

'Oh aye, so ye are,' he replied, and led me into the kitchen.

Only in the light of the kitchen did I now see that I had been standing in cow dung and leaning hard against the side of the animal with my shoulder. The animal, understandably, hadn't had a wash for some time, if ever. However, this didn't seem to matter to Rab, who was in a far worse state than me, having slipped in the mess of afterbirth and manure on his way out of the byre. He just barged on into the sitting room as he was, to introduce me to his wife, Ellen, who was sitting by the fire.

She looked wearily up at us as we entered the room.

'My God, Rab,' she wheezed. 'Whit have ye been daein wi' the doctor?'

I stopped, and half turned back to take my coat off, but Ellen stopped me.

'Don't worry, Doctor,' she said. 'I'll clean oot the place when I'm feeling a wee bit better.'

I walked over to her and began to ask about her illness. It soon became clear that she was much more ill than Rab suspected. She had pneumonia. It had affected both lungs, and she was not just breathless but going blue with the mildest exertion.

I had to decide what to do, fast. She should really have been in hospital, but the night was wild, the farm road very bumpy (Rab was not one for mending the potholes) and the hospital more than forty miles away. I felt that to keep her at home was the better option, provided she could have good nursing care. Rab wasn't exactly the ideal person to provide that.

First, I gave her an injection of penicillin and strepto-mycin – the best treatment then for pneumonia – and called Nurse Flora. She was with us in twenty minutes (her Morris Minor was slower than my Oxford, and she was a more careful driver), breezing into the room like a breath of fresh air. It was much needed, as by this time the warm farmhouse air had spread our miasma of cattle body fluids and worse throughout the room.

Flora took one look at me and grinned. Then she tended to Ellen. Luckily, Rab and Ellen's bedroom was on the ground floor, and Flora and I carried her into it and settled her into the double bed, arranging the pillows so that she could half lie, half sit up, in the most comfortable position for someone with pneumonia. Flora and I talked about how best she could be treated over the next few days, then we both returned just in time to see Rab walking out of the door – apparently to see how his new calf was doing.

Flora exploded. I witnessed something close to what the generals in the Crimea must have faced when confronted by Florence Nightingale after the battle of Balaclava. Flora told Rab in no uncertain terms that when she returned the next day, the kitchen and bedroom had to be spick and span, Ellen was to have had her breakfast and to be washed and resplendent in her best nightie. Rab was to arrange all that himself, and then he was to get someone in to look after her. Ellen was not to do a thing – 'no cooking, no housework, just nothing' – for at least three weeks. Rab, over six feet tall and not an ounce under eighteen stones, stood there and took this angry admonition from Flora, no more than five feet tall and seven and a half stones, in blushing silence.

I arrived at the house at eight-thirty the next morning to find a kitchen smelling of freshly cooked porridge and coffee that didn't resemble at all the room I had been standing in the night before. Ellen was sitting up in bed with a tray, tucking into a large brown soft-boiled egg and hot buttered brown toast, and already looking better.

Flora had been back in the middle of the night to give a second injection, and the antibiotics had obviously already done their stuff. There was no need to send Ellen to hospital. Rab, however, was nowhere to be seen. I asked Ellen where he was. Ellen, mouth full of egg, inclined her head towards the corridor that led off the bedroom. I wandered through to the guest bedroom, where I could hear heavy breathing. There was Rab, flat on his back, fast asleep, still with a kitchen cloth in his hand.

I walked back along the corridor to Ellen. She laughed when I explained how I had found Rab.

'He's been up all night cleaning and polishing and putting things right, and now he's exhausted. But there's an alarm clock there. Nurse Flora put it there and set it for eleven – that's when he's to bring me my coffee.'

Ellen recovered fully, and two months later, when she felt she could travel, she and Rab went for the first holiday together in their forty years of marriage.

There was another outcome of that visit to the Jackson house. Word soon spread that the doctor had helped to deliver a calf. Not long after its birth I was visiting an elderly lady, a Mrs Buchanan, on a farm near Braehill. It was a regular monthly call, more of a social visit than a medical one, and I always enjoyed a cup of tea with her. I had just raised the cup to my lips when her son Angus rushed in.

'While you're here, Doctor, could you come and see this? Maybe you could help?'

He showed me out of the house to the byre. Not again, I thought. I carefully studied the byre floor as I walked in behind him. It was covered with straw and reasonably clean. The cows, too, looked cleaner than Rab's.

We approached a single stall with a cow standing over a female calf that was lying in the straw, making no effort to rise. It wasn't difficult to see what was wrong. The calf's navel was opened, and the intestines were hanging out through it, still encased in the peritoneal sac – the membrane that surrounds the bowel. The condition in humans is called exomphalos: I presume vets call it the same.

'The mother has pulled too hard on the cord,' said Angus. 'It doesn't happen often. Maybe there's a weakness there. Can you do anything about it?'

'Shouldn't you call the vet?' I asked. 'It's more in his line.'

'There's no time for that,' he replied. 'The vet's in Ayr, and it would take more than an hour for him to get here. By that time, the calf will be dead – the bowel will swell up, and we won't be able to push it back. It'll get infected. We wouldn't be able to save it. I'll have to shoot it if we can't put the bowel back now.'

I swallowed and thought about it. I knew what to do. The surgery wasn't difficult. If I could push the intestine back without twisting or telescoping it, then sew the edges of the muscles and skin together, it could work, but I didn't have the tools to sew through tough animal skin. Mrs Buchanan solved that problem: despite her frailty, she had walked slowly to the byre door to find out why I was needed. She offered one of her strongest darning needles and Angus brought out a pack of fishing gut, and we were all set.

It was easier than I thought. The loops of bowel slid easily back into place, the edges of the muscles and skin came together nicely and smoothly, and Angus gave the animal a 'shot' of veterinary antibiotic to cover possible infection. The calf didn't react at all to the stitching, which suggested that she was unconscious. I needn't have worried. Within a few minutes she had already started to revive. I heard after that she thrived, and some two years later, on one of my regular visits, Mrs Buchanan proudly gave me my usual cup of tea, but this time with a drop of the calf's first sample of milk.

After this I began to get worried. There's a popular view that vets are allowed to treat sick humans, but that doctors are definitely not allowed to treat sick animals. I don't know that this is strictly true, but I do know that I didn't want to step on my vet friends' toes. I didn't want them to think I was usurping their place in our relatively restricted rural society.

Feeling like this, I took a lot of persuading before I performed my last act of animal therapy. It was the day of the Ayr Gold Cup, the biggest day in the West of Scotland racing calendar. I have to admit here that I wasn't fond of horses. They have big teeth at one end and nasty hooves at all four corners, all of which can inflict considerable damage to human soft tissues, and it wasn't long before, as a country doctor, I had to deal with more than my fair share of bites and kicks. I felt that if you were mad enough to ride them, you would inevitably fall off them, and then they could roll over you. I even thought they might well do that for spite, in a subtle reaction to all that kicking their sides to gee them on, or pulling at their mouths to slow them down.

My experience of tending to people who have been injured by these various equine attacks upon them made me shy away from close contact with horses. So Ayr Gold Cup day was a normal working day for me. I didn't expect it to be busy, because most of the population had decamped up to Ayr, dressed up and determined to enjoy themselves, leaving the Stinchar villages to philistines like myself.

Morning surgery attracted only a few regulars and the odd holidaymaker who had forgotten his pills, so I was able to start early on my routine visits for the day.

It was a beautiful morning, quiet, peaceful and sunny, and I drove slowly on the road inland from Collintrae towards a farm near Kilminnel, nestled in the centre of the valley, its fields stretching upwards to the hillside to the north.

The lady I was visiting, Eileen Rawson, had lived there all her life and was well into her seventies. Years of breathing in the dust from mouldy hay had finally got to her lungs, and she needed a lot of support to help her breathe. So Flora and I took it in turns to visit her once or twice a month to check on her. There wasn't much we could do for her physically, but the visits seemed to give her confidence, and we thought them worthwhile.

Mrs Rawson and I were chatting over the mandatory cup of tea – I must have drunk gallons of it on visits over the years – when there was a massive roar from outside. The farmhouse sat halfway up the valley, facing south. I turned my head towards the window just fast enough to catch a glimpse of a jet aircraft, exactly at my eye level, speeding like a bullet towards Collintrae.

The sudden noise had startled both of us. Mrs Rawson told me that this had just started to happen: the valley was being used for low-level flight training, and all the farmers along the flight path had been sent letters warning them about times and the noise. We settled back into our conversation for a while, then I rose to go. As my hand settled on the door handle, it was opened by someone from the outside.

It was Eric Rawson, Eileen's son. A slim, athletic man of around forty-five, he made his living, like most of his neighbours, from his lambs and beef cattle. But the loves of his life were his horses. He had ploughed with heavy horses as a young man, and when tractors replaced them he had turned them into a hobby. He bred hunters for point-to-pointers, show jumpers for three-day eventers and Clydesdales for professional ploughmen, and he loved them all.

He was looking for me, and was in a fury.

'That blasted jet,' he raged. 'Doc, seeing you're here, could you come and see Lowland Lad for me?'

I knew enough to recognise that Eric wasn't referring to a stable boy. In the yard, in a lather and wild-eyed was a very large horse, his reins being held firmly by Danny, Eric's handyman and groom. Danny was from Ireland, and apparently, what he didn't know about horses wasn't worth knowing. A retired National Hunt jockey, he had ridden several times in the Grand National. Danny was also in a sweat and breathing hard, but he was coolly trying to pacify the horse by whispering in his ear.

I could see at once why he and Eric were concerned.

233

Lowland Lad was bleeding freely from a cut about four inches long just above his left eyelid. The blood was flowing past the outer corner of his eye, down the side of his jaw and dripping onto the cobblestones at his feet.

'Do you think you could stitch it for us?' asked Eric.

'Stitch a HORSE?' I exclaimed. 'How would I keep it still when I put the needle in?'

Danny grinned and told me not to worry. He would guarantee to keep the horse quiet while I did it. And no, I wouldn't need to give a local anaesthetic.

'That horse has big teeth,' I said. 'How do you know it won't bite?' I asked him.

'We'll put a twitch on him,' he replied. 'All we want to know is, can you do it?'

'I really think this is a vet's job,' I said. 'Why don't you call him?'

Eric laughed. 'You do know it's Gold Cup day? All the vets are at the course. We wouldn't be able to get one till tomorrow.' I wondered where I had heard that before.

Lowland Lad did look a mess. There was a triangular flap of skin hanging over the upper eyelid, leaving the red flesh underneath exposed. It certainly wouldn't heal by itself without leaving a big scar, and the hanging skin would become infected and die off, possibly even endangering the horse's life. Someone would have to do something. I just wished it didn't have to be me.

'If you can guarantee that the horse will stand still, I can sew that flap back,' I said, with an outward optimism I didn't feel. I turned towards my emergency box and looked for the biggest suturing needle and strongest thread in it. While I was doing so, Eric told me that the horse had been 'spooked' by the sudden noise of the plane and had thrown his head back. His eyebrow had caught on a nail – for hanging tack at the side of the stall door – and this had ripped the skin.

As I prepared my materials, Danny produced a short piece of wood to which was tied a loop of smooth cord. Standing with his face at an angle to the horse's muzzle, he continued whispering into his ear. As he did so, he slowly slid the loop of cord around Lowland Lad's nose. When it was in exactly the right position, he tightened and rotated it, twisting and closing the nostrils.

Suddenly Lowland Lad was standing absolutely still. His eyes were no longer rolling, he just stood, looking straight ahead. Not even his tail moved.

'We're ready,' said Danny. 'Go ahead. He won't move until I loosen the twitch.'

Amazingly, that's exactly what happened. I washed out the torn area of flesh with sterile saline, and insert-ed the first stitch. Even when the needle pierced the thick skin, Lowland Lad didn't move – not an inch. I was able to insert five stitches to bring the flap and the surrounding skin edge together within less than a minute. When it was finished, the only sign that he had cut himself was the row of stitches. I washed off the blood and stood back. Danny removed the twitch, and Lowland Lad shook his head a little, but remained docile. Danny led him back to the stable to rest.

From then on, I looked on horses in a different light. Eric knew better than to offer me payment for the job, but he did offer me a riding lesson. Not on Lowland Lad, who would have been too lively a ride for a beginner, but on one of his Highland ponies, a docile and slow – and aged – nag who learned to tolerate me, and I him, reasonably well over the years.

Chapter Fifteen
Drunks – and Dead Drunks

The Scots are drunks: that's the reputation we have, and it's totally undeserved. All right, some of us get drunk some of the time, a few of us are drunk all the time, but quite a lot of us, more than half, in fact, have never been drunk at all. Our near-Puritan Presbyterianism ensures that just under half of all Scots, particularly in rural areas, are teetotal. I'm told that this is by far the biggest proportion of abstainers in any European nation. Another quarter of us feel so guilty about enjoying ourselves that we stick to the 'wee dram' each evening, and satiate the rest of our thirst with tea. It was the Scots, after all, who developed British tea drinking to a fine art, with Sir Thomas Lipton marketing the leaves that were grown and processed by the Findlay estates in Kenya and the Far East.

Tea, happily, causes little trouble for country doctors, except when we refuse yet another offer of a cup on our sixth house visit. Alcohol, on the other hand, is often a worry. I'm not writing here about drunken doctors (I have to draw the line somewhere) but about plastered patients. Over the years, Willie Tait, the Collintrae constable, and I had our share of them.

Fondness for alcohol has no social barriers: it afflicts the gentry, the farmers and their employees alike. The first may be more discreet, the second more devious, and the third wholly blatant about their addiction, but in the end it's the doctor who has to come to their rescue, provided they are willing to co-operate. Most of the time they aren't, but there is a time in every drunk's life when he (or she) has to face reality.

Willie rang me at eleven one Tuesday evening in June to say that he had been told there was a dead body on the South Shore Road, a few yards from its junction with the main road to Stranraer. Some holidaymakers, just arrived from England, had come across it on their way to the caravan park a mile further on. Could I meet him there?

It was only five minutes from the house, but even in

the short time it took us to get there, a small crowd had gathered beside the caravan which had managed to stop just in time. The body belonged to a man, who was lying face down, with one arm underneath his head and the other stretched out at a right angle to the torso. The legs were splayed apart.

In the grey light (it doesn't get completely dark in June on the Scottish west coast) Willie and I did not recognise the man until we were standing over him. As we bent down, we both heard a gentle snore. The man wasn't dead – he was dead drunk. We knew him well, of course. Jack Hunter lived in the first farmhouse on the road. His regular night out was always a Tuesday, after the weekly market in Ayr. Every Tuesday morning he and his stockman would drive the Hunter lorry filled with livestock the forty miles to Ayr, where they would sell their beasts and have lunch together at the Market Inn. The stockman would then pick up the new stock they had bought and drive them home, leaving Jack to enjoy the rest of the day with his cronies. They would bring him back in their truck when the Market Inn closed, which in those days of strict licensing was at ten o'clock sharp. By this time Jack was always well oiled.

Not wishing to incur the wrath of the formidable Jean, Jack's wife, Jack's mates were in the habit of leaving him about a hundred yards short of his gate. Most evenings, Jack would have been able to walk the rest of the way home, but not this time. He hadn't fallen or been knocked down: he had just found the road a good place to lie down, crook his head on his arm and fall asleep.

He roused a little when Willie and I moved him to check that there were no injuries, and we decided to help him home. We each took an arm and walked him, albeit unsteadily, towards the farmhouse. The crowd quickly dispersed, a bit disappointed that the body had turned out to be alive.

Arriving at the locked front door of a completely darkened house, we rang the bell and waited. A light snapped on in the room immediately above us, the sash and cord window was thrust upwards, and a roller-crowned head leaned out.

'Wha's there?' They were only two words but they imparted the instant message that Jean was not in the most benevolent of moods.

Willie decided to speak up. I was for taking the less than honourable option of leaving Jack on the doorstep and making a run for it.

'It's the polis and the doctor, Mrs Hunter. We've brought Jack home.'

Jean screwed up her eyes at these intruders on her doorstep. She didn't like what she saw. She sized us up for a while, then spoke.

'Well, ye canna leave him there, and he's no comin' inside ma hoose in that state. Jist pit him in the hayshed roon' the back. I'll see tae him in the mornin'.'

At that the window slammed shut and the light went out, leaving us in the dark and looking for the hayshed. Behind the house was the usual yard, beyond which was a long, low building with several wooden doors in it. We opened one of them and it was pitch black inside. With our torches left in the car for fear that they would encumber the task at hand, we had no idea what lay beyond the blackness but we were sure of one thing: we were not disturbing Jean again to find out where to put her husband.

Willie and I had to make a judgement. It was like one of the TV quiz shows of the day – which door hid the prize and which hid the forfeit? The smell of the first door suggested midden, so we tried the second. That smelled only marginally better, and was mixed with a strong smell of cow, so we tried the third. The air from that was much warmer and it smelled more of hay and straw than of animal. Willie and I looked at each other and helped Jack in. He was singing quietly to himself, not loudly enough to disturb Jean, so we judged that he was both conscious and comfortable, and sensible enough to know that he shouldn't disturb his good lady's sleep again that night.

We were pleased to find a heap of straw just inside the door and laid Jack on it. As we left him, he started snoring loudly, so we tiptoed out, content with our night's work, and shut the door behind us.

Waking up the next morning, I wasn't quite so sure we had done the correct thing. Was it really acceptable to have left him in such a state? I decided to drive back to the farm before surgery started, to make sure he had survived the night. When I drove up to the farmhouse door I was immediately aware of a commotion going on behind the house, in the yard. I got out of the car and walked round the corner to see Jean with a hose, turned full on and directed straight at a dejected, forlorn and naked Jack, who was standing over the sunken drain in the middle of the yard, with the water cascading off him.

The redoubtable Jean saw me and stopped the hose for a moment. She turned to me and gave me full voice.

'Why did ye pit ma husband in the pigpen?' she blasted. 'That wisnae the hayshed. Look at him – and his claes. I'll hae to dump them.'

I looked at a pile of what seemed to be rags lying in a corner of the yard. Examined more closely there was a brown suit, a shirt and long johns. For some unfathomable reason, Mrs Hunter had allowed her spouse to put his boots back on. She had obviously had to remove them to take off his long johns.

I walked over to the door of the shed where we had left him. There was the pig, a huge pink pregnant beast, lying in the heap of straw. Beside her was the Jack-shaped depression where we had laid him the night before. The sow was snoring: it became quickly clear to me that the snores we had heard the previous night had come from her and not a human throat. Why hadn't we smelled her? Our sense of smell, of course, wanes after a few moments when assailed by strong odours. We had smelled the midden first and the cows second. By the time we had come to the pig, our noses were tired – and rightly so.

I turned to Jack and Jean. I had to work very hard not to smile at our mistake, as Jean was very definitely not amused.

'Whit am ah goin' tae dae wi' these claes?' she asked, reasonably. I suggested the dry cleaners in Girvan. They had made a good job of cleaning my clothes: perhaps they could do the same for her.

Jean walked over to the heap and picked up the jacket.

'Dae ye think that they'll tak' claes like this?' she asked. 'I dinna think sae.'

She wasn't wrong. The straw hadn't exactly been clean. And in staggering around in the pen, Jack had fallen over the animal. His clothes were not just stained but torn. They were irretrievable.

And then Jean suddenly winked at me and a suspicion of a grin flitted across her face.

'I want ye tae come inside for a minute,' she said. 'Follow me. And you,' she said, talking to Jack, 'ye'd better get in and hae a hot bath.'

The three of us walked into the house, Jack up to the bathroom, Jean and I into the front room, where we sat down in armchairs either side of the fireplace.

She listened to the bathroom door shutting and then leaned across at me and beamed. 'Thanks, Doctor, for giving me the biggest laugh of my life,' she said. You and Constable Tait helped a lot last night, and I'm grateful. Maybe he'll stop drinking for a while and stop making an ass of himself. He's done it before after a shock like this.'

And after a shock like this one, Jack did indeed alter, but not in a direction anyone had expected. I've got two

'I walked round the corner to see Jean with a hose, turned full on, and directed straight at a dejected, forlorn and naked Jack... For some unfathomable reason, Mrs Hunter had allowed her spouse to put his boots back on.'

theories about that. Asclepius, the founder of medicine centuries before Hippocrates, swore by the benefits of dropping agitated and depressed patients into pits full of snakes to shock them back into health. Waking up hung over and with no memory of the night before, sprawled across a heavily pregnant pig, could have had the same effect. On the other hand, standing naked in a yard before breakfast being hosed down with cold water could be compared with ECT.

Whatever the cause, Jack eschewed alcohol from that day onwards. Sadly, his personality wasn't strong enough for him to avoid replacing it with another addiction. He adopted religion instead. Jack didn't do his addictions by halves, and it wasn't long before he was a regular on the lay-preacher circuit, thundering on street corners and in his old haunts against the evils of alcohol.

The second in my portfolio of memorable Stinchar Valley drunks was Patrick Flannigan. Patrick was brought into Willie's house, which doubled as his home and the police station, by a local lorry driver in the early hours of a Sunday morning. He had been picked up staggering about the road north of Collintrae, where it ran by the beach. He was shivering, which was not surprising, because he was soaked to the skin, and he was rambling on about being shown the right road to Belfast.

The driver found the answer to that question a tad difficult because to get to the Belfast road meant first driving to Stranraer thirty miles to the south, taking the ferry across the Irish Channel to Larne, then picking it up from there. This was clearly a problem for Willie the polis to sort out.

Willie didn't see it as part of his job to unravel a drunken man's confusion: his sole interest was to make sure that he wasn't ill before he banged Patrick up for the night as drunk and disorderly. Drunk he certainly was. Disorderly was another matter. He was a mess, right enough, and needed warming up and dry clothing, but he seemed harmless and no threat to anyone. Unless he had been at the wheel of a car. So how had he come to be wandering the road over here?

Patrick was co-operative and truthful. He had driven in his black Ford Anglia from Belfast to Larne, where his brother worked and lived on the ferry. It had been his brother's night off, but he had held a party in the bar on the boat, and Patrick had been the guest of honour. During the party, the boat had made one of its round trips between Larne and Stranraer, time enough for Patrick to enjoy a few drinks. He had then disembarked at Larne, got into his car, and driven off back to Belfast.

At this point in the tale, Patrick had frowned. He

must have taken a wrong turning, he said, because the road back to Belfast seemed unfamiliar, but he reckoned that if he kept the sea on his left-hand side, he was bound to hit the town. After all, Larne and Belfast were on the same stretch of the east coast of Ulster, and the coast road was bound to lead to the city. Unfortunately, after a few miles he seemed to have missed a bend, and the next thing he knew he was in the sea, and climbing out of his car onto the road. That's where he was when he had been picked up.

It was then that Willie decided to phone me, utterly bemused by Patrick. The man was not only drunk; if his story was correct he was also the first person to swim the fifty miles across the Irish Channel fully clothed, four sheets to the wind, in the hours of darkness. There was an alternative of course: he could be an absconder from a psychiatric hospital.

But Willie was an old-fashioned and kindly police-man. Annie, his wife, hunted out some of his old clothes for Patrick to wear and gave him some strong coffee. Willie and I then drove out to the spot where the driver had found him. There were marks of tyres tearing across the machair, leading straight to the sea. It was still too dark to see anything clearly, so Willie said he'd return to the spot in the morning and sort things out. Patrick remained in the hospitality suite in the police station – the only cell – and we had to figure out what had happened.

It became clear the next day. One of the crew of the ferry was based in Stranraer and drove each day to the ship in his black Ford Anglia, which he parked on the dockside. He left his keys in it: nobody stole cars in those days. It appeared that the party had gone on longer than Patrick had thought. He had made three crossings, not two. The third had, of course, ended in Stranraer, which he had mistaken for Larne. His less than coherent brain had spotted the Anglia, the same colour and model as his own, and drawn the wrong conclusion. For the first few miles the road north along the Scottish west coast looks similar to the road south along the Ulster east coast. Sober, nobody would have confused the two, but drunk anything's possible.

That morning Willie found the black Anglia where he expected it, in the sea. And that evening a sober and extremely penitent Patrick delivered his car, keys and all, to the crew member whose car he had taken. It was a fair exchange. He pleaded guilty to driving under the influence and was banned for a year. The man whose car he had inadvertently stolen pleaded successfully with the justice of the peace to let Patrick off the more serious charge of car theft, adding that he now had a better vehicle, thanks to Patrick's generosity.

Cars were also the problem that brought notable Stinchar Valley drunk number three into my care. Steven Williamson was a self-made man, a farmer who had worked hard in his youth, building up the best beef and dairy herds in the district. What he didn't know about the relative merits of Aberdeen Angus and Galloways, Ayrshires and Holsteins wasn't worth knowing. The farming establishment, recognising his preeminence in such matters, invited him on this national board and that international committee, and paid for him to visit places all over the world, from East Africa to South America, to oversee the proper management of their exported British cattle blood lines.

Less well known was that he had a similarly encyclopaedic grasp of the merits of the Scottish glens, names such as Glenmorangie, Glenfiddich, Glenlivet and Glengoyne often appearing on his shopping list. He was not at all averse to sampling their end-products generously and at any time of day. His wife Isabel kept this secret until the day that she and Steven celebrated a recent success at the Perth bull sales by buying new cars.

On the way home from Perth, they stopped off in Glasgow to trade in their Rover for a top-of-the-line Fiat for the family and an Alpha-Romeo runabout for Isabel. Italian cars were all the rage then, and where fashion went, the Williamsons were never far behind. Isabel drove home ahead, with Steven following, although Steven's car dropped out of Isabel's rear-view mirror when they were about halfway home. Which is why Isabel had already parked her pride and joy and had put a pot of tea on the kitchen table when Steven roared up the drive. Their house was on a hill, and it took a little acceleration to push the car up the last steep slope and around the corner into the yard beside the kitchen window.

Far be it from me to criticise either Steven's reaction time on the day, or Isabel's wisdom in parking her Alpha under the kitchen window, where she could admire it while enjoying a refreshing cup of Lipton's best. Whoever was at fault, the result was that Steven turned the corner too fast, and the two new cars were written off in a fraction of a second.

Steven got away with a large bruise on his forehead and a distinctly wounded pride. As the accident had occurred on his own driveway, there was no need for the police to be involved, but I was called to make sure that he wasn't seriously hurt.

The examination didn't reveal any physical injury, but

251

I was struck, when examining his eyes, that the whites were a bit more yellow than they should have been. I presumed that this was an effect of the room lighting, and asked him to come to the kitchen window to see him in daylight. They were still yellow.

I wasn't happy with this, and asked him to go through into the bedroom to let me look at him more thoroughly. The after-examination discussion with the Williamsons was straightforward. Steven was to come to the surgery the following day for blood tests to check on his liver. I couldn't be sure, but I thought he might have a touch of jaundice, and that had to be followed up.

A few days later, Isabel arrived at the surgery on her own. For the first time she revealed the extent of Steven's drinking. He kept swearing that he would stop, but he hid bottles in the fields, in hay lofts, under machinery, anywhere he thought she wouldn't find them. He was now feeling sick most days and was too weak to get up out of bed for more than a few hours in the afternoons. Could I possibly give him a fright, to stop him before it was too late? I didn't need to put on an act to give him a fright, I said to her. His liver function tests were enough to frighten anyone. They showed severe alcoholic liver damage. If he didn't stop drinking alcohol, he would soon be in liver failure. In those days,

years before dedicated liver disease teams and trans-
plants, that meant a fairly rapid death. I would be happy,
I said, to come to see him at home and read him the Riot
Act.

'I'm not sure he would listen to you alone,' she said.
'He thinks you're just a wee boy. Could you get someone special, with a medical reputation, to see him? He
respects real authority.'

I could understand that. Mr Williamson thought of
himself as an authority, and wanted an equal as his physician, not a youngster like myself. I wasn't sure who that
might be in our region. It would have been easy in
Birmingham: there, I could have named three or four
consultant physicians with just the right air of superior-
ity and medical gravitas to impress him. There wasn't
such a medical hierarchy in Ayrshire. All the consultants
who served our district, who were based mainly in Ayr,
were brilliant physicians but straightforward, down-to-
earth men and women with no hint of pomposity. I
would have to cast my net further afield, probably as far
as Glasgow for someone to fit Isabel's needs.

I phoned Arthur Thomson, my colleague from Darley
and a Glasgow graduate, and he came up with the name
of Dr Jonas Hall, a famous gastroenterologist who had
deeply impressed him as a student, not so much for his

knowledge of diseases and their cures, but for the collection of Rolls-Royces that he had managed to acquire in the course of his private practice.

Dr Hall was obviously the man for the Williamsons.

I spoke to his secretary on the phone. The doctor was slightly indisposed today, she told me, but he would be delighted to make a 'private' home visit. The fee would be high because the round trip would be more than a hundred miles, but that could be an advantage, she suggested, if the patient needed to be impressed.

What a wise secretary, I thought, and agreed to put the proposal to Isabel. She jumped at it.

'Just the thing, Doctor,' she said. 'I'll break the news to Steven that he is being seen privately by the most prestigious liver doctor in the West of Scotland.'

I wasn't sure that this was the way I had described Dr Hall, but I let it go at that.

When he arrived three days later, it was certainly with a flourish. I had been in the house only a minute or so when his Roller glided up the steep driveway to the front door. There was no corner to negotiate and no danger of colliding with the Williamsons' replacement car. A chauffeur with peaked cap and smart grey suit got out and with appropriate dignity opened the rear driver's side door.

Out stepped the great doctor. His eminence could be seen at a glance. Most of it was round his middle. There was the grey morning suit like the men wear at Ascot on Ladies' Day, and the shoes with spats. A picture of James Robertson Justice as the terrifying professor in *Doctor in the House* flashed into my mind.

'Dr Smith? So good to meet you. Thank you for asking me to see this most interesting patient,' he said. In a second flash, Uriah Heap replaced James Robertson Justice. I was in for a show, not a consultation.

We turned to enter the house. I took a closer look at my colleague as we walked along the hall towards the bedroom, where Mr Williamson was waiting ready to be examined. He was certainly in ruddy health, to judge by the rose-red cheeks and, for that matter, nose. The bulging waistcoat and triple chin suggested a gourmet lifestyle and a certain lack of exercise. He was a bit clumsy, too. Was that a slight stumble as he walked up the steps? Did his words sound a little slurred? I dismissed these thoughts as scurrilous and walked forward to introduce him to our hosts.

Our patient, in preparation for the visit, had abstained from hard liquor for a day, a feat that had cleared his head and his vision for the first time in months. He responded to Dr Hall's questions and to his probing examination in a sober and even subdued manner. He lay back on the pillows at the end and waited for the verdict.

Dr Hall brought out a sheet of paper from his document case. He showed it to our patient and asked him to note very carefully the figures on it. He then brought out a book with a marker at a page near the end and asked Mr Williamson to compare them. I was curious and looked over Dr Hall's shoulder at the two pages. On the paper were the liver function results, in the book were similar figures presented as examples of liver failure. They were close to identical.

'If you don't stop drinking,' warned Dr Hall in his most severe tone, 'you are heading very fast for cirrhosis and an early death. I want to see you in Glasgow in two months' time, in my rooms, and I want these results to be far better by then.'

At that the great man rose to go. As he walked back to his car, he swayed, just a little. He refused any refreshment and was soon on his chauffeur-driven way back to Glasgow.

The next day, I returned to the Williamson house. Steven was sitting up. He still hadn't had a drink and seemed keen to take this change seriously.

'Don't worry, Doc,' he said. 'I'm on the wagon.

I'll do what I'm told.'

'So those figures shocked you,' I said. 'I thought they might. That was the idea.'

'It wasn't the figures, Doc. It was him. Dr Hall.'

'Pardon?'

'He didn't know me, but I knew him,' Steven said. 'We're members of the same club – the RAC club in Glasgow. I've seen him sitting over his brandies there, in a corner, and his chauffeur waiting for him outside in the car. You know why he has a chauffeur? He's banned from driving. He's a lush. When he bent over me, I could smell the booze on his breath. I suddenly thought, "Is this what I'll be like?" I decided I didn't want that, so I'm stopping.'

Sadly, Dr Hall didn't fare so well. A year later he died. Many of his obituaries in the press, national and medical, referred to the great contributions he had made to gastroenterology, and most to his special interest in alcoholic liver disease, but each one without fail referred to his 'larger than life, jovial' personality.

CHAPTER SIXTEEN
DID SHE, OR DIDN'T SHE?

Elsie Turner was in her mid-thirties when I first got to know her. Tall, slim, with brown eyes matching her hair, and the even features of a model, she had the sort of looks that made both women and men stop, just for an instant, when she entered a room. She was the beauty of the district, and she made sure everyone knew it. At the parish meetings, the Women's Guild and the Conservative party coffee mornings she was always the star. At church on Sundays, she was the last to enter, her high heels taking her elegantly past the rest of the congregation to her reserved pew at the front. She made a point of settling into her place just before the entrance of the minister. She was most definitely there to be seen.

Elsie was the last of her line, but it was not a Collintrae line. She had known the village all her life, the only daughter of parents who had had a holiday house there from before she was even born. She could well have been conceived there, but that didn't make her or her family natives. The Turners remained 'incomers' even after they had sold their Edinburgh home, when Mr Turner retired, to move permanently to Collintrae.

Mr Turner had been someone in the City (which in Scotland, of course, means Edinburgh), and over the years had spared no expense in improving, extending, decorating and furnishing his Collintrae property, until it was the most luxurious house in the village.

Or so rumour had it. Unfortunately, few people had the chance to confirm whether this was so. The older Turners were not gregarious and held no soirées or dinner parties. And if they were intending to hold them, their plans were cut short when Mr Turner died suddenly only a month into his too-short retirement. From then on, Elsie, now in her mid-twenties, had had to look after her mother, Catherine.

By the time I arrived in the village, ten years after Mr Turner's death, Catherine was in great physical difficulties. A small, very thin, frail woman, she had had a severe form of arthritis for years that had affected her spine, hips and knees, so that she could only shuffle around the house. With a stick in each hand to take the weight from her legs, she moved one foot in front of her about six inches, then painfully dragged the other next to it. She had to repeat this dozens of times to go from the dining room to the kitchen, and again to the bathroom, the living room and her bedroom, all of which had been moved to the ground floor. Her neck vertebrae had fused into a solid mass, so that her head was rigidly set and could not swivel on her shoulders. To see to either side she had to turn her whole body, a very difficult manoeuvre while she was standing and impossible when seated.

To make matters worse, the lack of movement in her joints and under-use of her muscles had made her bones very brittle. Two years before she had broken a wrist simply by putting too much weight on it when rising from a chair, and any slip or fall would surely result in a more serious fracture, perhaps of a hip. She did the best she could, but needed constant help to attend to even her smallest needs. It meant that Elsie was fully occupied with her from morning to night. Elsie's haven was a small sitting room and bedroom upstairs, to which she would escape whenever she could, usually only when her mother was asleep. Even then she was at the call of a bell that her mother would ring when she needed her.

Nurse Flora came in to give a hand as often as her busy schedule permitted, but it was only a fraction of the burden that fell on Elsie's shoulders. I asked Catherine one day why she didn't employ a woman from the village to help her, and to give Elsie a break, but she didn't see the need. Elsie was family and she didn't want anyone from the village in the house – apart, of course, from nurse, doctor and minister.

I visited the Turner house every week, more often if the old lady was in pain and needed injections, but was frustrated by being unable to organise more help, mainly to give Elsie a rest, rather than to please Catherine. It wasn't long before I realised there was an undercurrent of anger simmering between them. The younger woman resented that she had no permissible social life because of her total commitment to her mother's health. The older woman, although outwardly kind and generous (she was the biggest donor to church funds and to all the local charities), was blind to the fact that her daughter was growing older and sacrificing the chance of a life of her own. For her the prime function of a daughter was to look after her parent: there could be no argument about that. She made sure, from time to time, in blazing rows, that Elsie understood.

So life had gone on for the two women, the younger one becoming more frustrated and the older one more ill and incapacitated as the years passed. They were isolated from the society that they had been used to in Edinburgh and, still clinging to the Edwardian ideas of social class, had never brought themselves down to the level of making close friends of the villagers. It was one thing to mix with them at charity or church functions, in fact, it was their duty to do so, but quite another to invite them home.

There were rumours, however, that Elsie was not the slave to her mother that she appeared. It was said that she was living a double life, and that she had 'friends' whom she would meet late in the evenings. The house was built on a slope so that at the back there was a short outside staircase leading directly to the first floor and Elsie's self-contained flat. Behind the house there was a convenient wooded area, through which anyone walking late at night could reach the staircase without the need to pass by the front door. Anyone could walk through the woods, and a surprising number of men had dogs to exercise in the evenings.

The village wives, naturally, were suspicious of her, and their worries were reinforced by memories of Elsie's conquests at village dances in her younger days.

She had been known as a flirt and a tease, and there were darker mutterings that she did more than tease.

Of course none of this reached my ears: no one carried gossip to the doctor or the doctor's wife. We, too, were incomers, and not privy to the village gossip; but actually much of the distance between us and the villagers was of our own making. It's best not to become too friendly with your patients in a single-handed practice. There always comes a time when the doctor has to make a serious decision for a patient, and it's crucial that friendship or an emotional attachment does not interfere with clinical judgment. A plea from a friend in a crisis not to send him into hospital is more difficult to resist than a plea from a patient who is socially a stranger. It's best for doctors to find their closest friends among people outside their practice. A result of this was, of course, that we missed a lot of what was going on in the village, and thus it was that the growing problems in the Turner house escaped me.

Twice a year, Mairi and I and the two children took a fortnight's holiday. We had to book a locum doctor for those two weeks, because we felt it wrong to ask Dr Jimmy to stand in for so long. He was an excellent stand-in for a day or two at a time, but he was over sixty-five and a two-week stretch without a break was an unfair burden on him. So we used to advertise in one of the medical papers, and were generally delighted with the response from a host of young doctors willing to take on the country practice as a break from busy hospitals or city practices. On this occasion we chose the one who seemed the most experienced and enthusiastic and looked forward to him arriving. The day before we left, I visited the Turners. I wanted to make sure that Mrs Turner had all the drugs she needed for the month ahead, and to tell them about the locum. It was a warm summer's day, and the windows on the ground floor were open. As I walked up the drive to the front door I could hear, through one of the windows, voices raised in anger. Yet when Elsie opened the door to me, all was sweetness and light. The two women welcomed me, Catherine seated in her usual armchair, Elsie perched on one arm, as if they had never had a cross word. I talked to them both for a while, gave Elsie the pack of medicines, checked on Catherine's pulse and blood pressure and left.

On our return from holiday, my locum was waiting for me. He had a list of patients he had seen, and had certainly kept up a high standard of practice. There had only been one death, he said – a Mrs Catherine Turner.

This was a surprise. She was frail, but there was

nothing to predict an impending sudden death.

'What happened?' I asked. 'Did she have a heart attack or a stroke? Her blood pressure and pulse were OK when I last saw her.'

'No, it was just an unfortunate accident,' he replied. 'She fell downstairs. Her daughter found her in the morning, just two days after you left. She was in a crumpled heap at the bottom of the stairs. Her neck was broken. She had such advanced osteoporosis I suppose any fall might have caused that – especially if it was down a staircase.'

I couldn't believe what I was hearing.

'But she couldn't have been on a stair. She couldn't lift either foot more than an inch off the floor. She would never have attempted to go upstairs. Did you report the sudden death?'

'Sure,' he replied. 'I phoned the Procurator Fiscal and gave him all the details. I had your notes to say that she had advanced osteoporosis, and that you had seen her just two days before. He asked if I thought there could be any cause for suspicion of anything more than an accident, and I didn't. So he allowed me to sign the death certificate and the cremation forms.'

'The cremation forms?' I asked. 'But everyone gets buried here. The cemetery is just outside the village: the nearest crematorium is in Ayr, forty miles away. Who asked for cremation?'

'Her daughter, Elsie. She said that the family had always been for cremation, rather than burial, and that was her mother's wish.'

'Who signed the second part?' I asked. 'Was it Jimmy Anderson?'

'No, Jimmy was away for a few days. I got one of the Stranraer doctors to do it. He's an old friend. He came to see the body and agreed that the injuries were compatible with an accident. Why are you asking all these questions? You don't think Elsie could have had something to do with her death, surely?'

'I'm not sure,' I said. 'But if she has been cremated, we can't do anything about another opinion now. If she killed her mother, she has got away with it.'

My locum was shocked. 'I'm sorry,' he said. 'I just didn't think there could be anything abnormal about this death. Her daughter seemed perfectly nice and so fond of her mother. I find it hard to believe that she might have done anything to harm her'.

'Then maybe you should have a conversation with her father about it,' I said.

'What do you mean?' he asked. 'Didn't he die ten years ago?'

'Yes,' I replied. 'He is lying in the Collintrae grave-yard, just a mile away. His widow buried him. Curious, isn't it, that she didn't want to lie beside him?'

Could Elsie be harbouring a disturbed personality behind her charming façade? I resolved to be very care-ful in my dealings with her from then on.

The death of her mother let her spread her wings more widely, and she began to live a little. There's an old story about the minister who had lost his bicycle. Convinced it had been stolen by one of his flock, he asked the parish clerk how he might retrieve it without involving the police. The clerk suggested that he preach a sermon on the Ten Commandments, and that when he got to 'thou shalt not steal', he should pause for a moment and scan the faces of the faithful. The guilty one among them would not fail to blush and so give himself away. On the following Sunday the clerk was surprised to hear the minister rattling through the Ten Commandments without stopping. Curious about this, he asked the minister afterwards why he had not paused at the appropriate commandment. It was simple, said the minister. When he got to 'thou shalt not commit adultery', he remembered where he had left his bike.

Apparently, there were bicycles aplenty – needless to say, not the minister's – to be seen from time to time leaning against Elsie's back door. She was shameless in making up for her wasted years. After a few months, the bicycles became fewer, and one car in particular started to grace her drive.

Its owner lived a few miles away, near Braehill, in a substantial estate house. Angus Marshall was an early retiree from the city, who had known the Turners when they lived in Edinburgh. Twenty years older than Elsie, and fifteen years younger than her parents, he had been like an older brother or a relatively young uncle to her – or so she told me, one day as I was renewing her prescription. Since her mother's death, she had had to have the contraceptive pill, not for contraceptive purposes of course, but to 'regulate her periods'. She was entering that certain age for women, she said, and wanted to make certain that it went smoothly.

Mr Marshall was helping her out with her financial problems, she said, which was why his car was so often in front of her house. Why she had to tell me this I wasn't sure. It struck me as unnecessary, and perhaps a small sign that she was feeling guilty about something.

The Marshalls were also patients of mine. He was fit and physically active, being part of a syndicate of farmers and estate owners who reared and shot pheasants and grouse on the hillside behind his home. He also owned a stretch of Cree water on which to indulge his passion for salmon and sea trout fishing. The Cree runs south from the hills around Braehill through Newton Stewart to the Solway. It is the neighbouring river to the Stinchar, and the locals argue interminably without ever reaching a conclusion about their relative merits.

However, Angus Marshall's main activity was to look after his sick wife. Olive Marshall suffered from what was then called 'pre-senile dementia' and is now better known as Alzheimer's disease. By the time I took over her care – I visited her once a month, and Nurse Flora dropped in once a week – the disease was in its middle stages. She was careless about her looks, found it diffi-cult to remember things, was neglecting the housework and cooking and had given up almost all of her social activities. Friends did visit, but were calling less and less often because she had so little to say and was too con-fused to recognise them or appreciate their company. Angus organised for a woman to stay with her several times a week, so that he could have some freedom. Visiting Elsie was one of these 'freedoms'.

A year after her mother died, I was due my next summer holiday, and had yet again to employ a doctor to stand in. My locum of the previous year was now in a practice of his own and was unavailable, so I had to advertise again. This time a young woman was the most suitable, and both Mairi and I were thrilled when she accepted the job.

In the usual way, I discussed with her the care of the various people she would have to visit, one of whom was Olive Marshall. She said she would be delighted to look in on her, and I left for our holiday in Cornwall happy that the practice was in safe hands.

On my return, she told me that there had been one death while I was away – Olive Marshall. This time I wasn't too surprised, because dementia often takes people suddenly, when one isn't really expecting it. What did surprise me was how the death had happened.

Apparently, Olive had gone missing the evening after my departure on holiday. She had walked out of the door late in the evening when the lady looking after her had been preparing her bath, and had had her attention diverted by a phone call. After a frantic search through the night, Olive had been found next morning facedown in the small stream beside the house. Like so many other streams running off the hillside, it had carved out a steep mini-ravine for itself, and anyone falling over the edge would hit the rocks a good ten feet below. In her precarious state she had no chance of surviving. Her skull was fractured, and there were clear marks down the side of the bank where she had obviously fallen. She was in her nightshirt and slippers, corroborating the story of the lady looking after her.

'Who was this lady?' I asked.

'A Miss Turner' was the reply.

'Elsie Turner?' I asked. 'Was she upset?'

'Very. She needed sedation after the body was found. She kept on blaming herself. She said she had searched all night, but hadn't been able to see down into the stream.'

'Where was Mr Marshall at the time?' I asked.

'He had gone to Glasgow to meet up with friends. Apparently, Miss Turner had suggested he needed a night away and offered to look after his wife. She was devastated that this had happened.'

I'll bet she was, I thought. How convenient that on the two occasions when the resident doctor was away there had been two accidental deaths that impinged so directly on her life. Did she think that I would have taken things much further than a locum might?

'Did you inform the Procurator Fiscal?' I asked.

'There was no need,' she said. 'There were police everywhere the next day, first hunting for her and then, after she was found, looking for evidence of foul play.'

'And was there any?'

'No. There had been a lot of footprints in the grass just above where she fell into the stream, but they were explained. Apparently, Miss Turner had been walking there the previous evening looking for her, with no success.'

'So it was put down as an accidental death?'

'Yes.'

Once my locum had gone, I telephoned the Procurator Fiscal's office. He had taken his holiday at the same time as I had, and a locum Fiscal had been in place when the accident had been investigated. No one had made any connection between the two deaths, and there was still no reason to connect them. The consensus was that they were just a sad coincidence for Miss Turner, and there was little point in stirring things further.

I thought about it for a while, then let it drop. Nothing I could do would bring the two women back, and any interference from me would only raise unpleasant, unprovable suspicions. Reluctantly, I decided to leave well alone.

A year later, Elsie Turner and Angus Marshall married discreetly in an Edinburgh church, far from Ayrshire. They returned to live in his mansion on the banks of the Cree, the spot where Olive had died in full view of their lounge window.

Over the next thirty years, I had no occasion to be involved with them until she was in her sixties and he in his eighties, when I was no longer in full-time practice. Angus Marshall telephoned me one evening when I was the duty doctor in the Ayrshire 24-hour On-Call service. He was glad it was me. Could he possibly come to see me at my home, that evening?

He arrived about half an hour after the call. He was older and had more worry lines etched into his face, but he was still lean and fit.

I welcomed him into our lounge and sat him down with a small whisky.

'I'm not sure if you can help us,' he said, 'but I don't know who else can. You see, you have known Elsie longer and probably better than anyone. There may be something you can say or do that can rid her of her nightmares.'

'Nightmares?' I asked.

'For years she has been depressed. She mopes about the house worrying and muttering. In the last few months,' he continued, 'she has been having terrible nightmares. She wakes up terrified and doesn't want to go back to sleep, in case the nightmare starts again.'

'Has she seen a psychiatrist?' I asked.

'She won't see one,' he replied. 'She says there's

nothing anyone can do for her.'

'She hasn't tried to harm herself?'

'That's the funny thing. She is so depressed that my sister, who was a psychiatric nurse, did ask her whether she had thoughts of suicide. At that she went right off the rails, shouting that it would only precipitate her into hell. Do you think you could come to see her, in a private visit, some time?'

I thought about that for a few minutes.

'Does she know you have come to see me?' I asked.

'Good God, no,' he said. 'I'm doing this off my own bat. She would be furious if she thought I'd asked you.'

'Then maybe I'm the wrong man, Angus. If she needs help from me she needs to ask for it herself. She really needs a minister or a truly expert psychiatrist. I'll give you a few names, but if you would like her to see me please ask her first. I'll come if she says yes.'

The invitation never came. Instead the next day at about ten o'clock in the morning their doctor telephoned me. I wasn't surprised, because she would have received my faxed records of the conversation when she came on duty the next morning.

'Hi Tom,' she said. 'I see you spoke to Angus Marshall last night.'

'Yes, though it was really about his wife, not himself.'

'I understand that. But did you hear what happened later?'

'No.'

'You are sitting down, aren't you?'

'Yes – why?'

'Elsie took a kitchen knife to him this morning. Just after he said he had been to see you.'

'What? How do you know?'

'He told us. Luckily, she isn't very strong and her aim wasn't good, so she only pierced his shoulder and missed anything vital. He was able to subdue her, and she's in the Arran.'

The Arran is our emergency psychiatric unit.

I never discovered why Elsie became so upset about his meeting with me – but I think I can make a guess that's not too wide of the mark.

CHAPTER SEVENTEEN
'TWAS CHRISTMAS DAY IN THE PRACTICE, AND THE PATIENTS ALL SAT ON THE STAIRS...

Christmas Day wasn't a holiday in Scotland in the Sixties. I learned that the hard way. Assuming that no one would expect a surgery on my first Christmas Day, I walked downstairs that morning in my dressing gown and slippers to make coffee and toast, to find six men waiting in the hall. It was only two months after moving into the Collintrae house, the planned waiting room wasn't yet ready, and the hall had had to do in the meantime. It was comfortable enough, with a Rayburn stove and plenty of chairs. The overflow could sit on the stairs if they wished – in fact, two of them were doing just that.

The men clearly expected me to be working as usual and, as some of them had come several miles, I didn't want to disappoint them. I quickly ran upstairs, put on my clothes and arrived, a bit breathless, a few minutes later, to start the surgery. No one bothered about this strange behaviour, presumably because the young doctor from England was still a bit green, and didn't know the rules.

What I hadn't known was that for most of the men, Christmas Day was their only official break from their duties as dairymen or shepherds, at least at my normal surgery times. It was the one day in their year in which they could grab an opportunity to do important things – like seeing their doctor.

That was Christmas 1965. From then on I did hold a surgery on Christmas morning, but I let nurse Flora spread around in her masterful way that it was for emergencies only. As each Christmas passed and the social climate changed, there were fewer and fewer Christmas attendees.

On Christmas Day 1967, I had just one patient to see. He brought in a problem quite unlike any other I have ever had. Charlie Welsh was the physics teacher at the local academy in Girvan. He was good at his job, because the school had excellent 'Highers' results, with many of

'...on my first Christmas Day, I walked downstairs in my
dressing gown and slippers to make coffee and toast,
to find six men waiting in the hall...'

the pupils, boys and girls, going on to study science at university. His real love, however, was birds. Every day, before driving the fourteen miles to the school, he would walk a few miles along the shingle beach, noting the numbers, types and behaviour of the birds he saw. The shingle bank to the north of the mouth of the River Stinchar is home to nesting terns, and it was to Charlie's credit that it was made a Site of Special Scientific Interest and protected for the foreseeable future.

That Christmas Day, Charlie sat down in the surgery and pulled out a package from the inside pocket of his overcoat. He unwrapped it to reveal a dead grey-backed gull.

'What do you make of this, Doc?' he asked.

'Well, Charlie, it seems to be dead,' I said, grinning at him. 'I'm not sure I'm qualified to tell you more.'

'There are thousands more like it on the beach,' he said. 'And it's not just grey-backs. There are fulmars, kittiwakes, black-backs, shags and cormorants – all of them dead. They've appeared in the last two or three days. There are a few still alive and staggering around, choking as if they can't breathe. They have bubbles of mucus around their mouths, and I could swear that some of them are coughing.'

I looked at the dead bird again. I was obviously no

expert, but the mouth was flecked with mucus and even tiny spots of blood.

'I suppose they could have some form of pneumonia,' I said, 'with bleeding into their lungs, but I've no way of telling. Why don't you let the vets know?'

'They aren't interested in dead gulls,' he said. 'They'd just laugh. I wondered if you'd be able to throw any light on them.'

'I don't know that I can, short of doing a post-mortem on it, and even then I wouldn't know what I was looking for. And I'd be a bit concerned about close contact with the bird's tissues. It could be botulism – poisoning from scavenging on the rubbish tips when sea food is low. I wouldn't want to expose myself or you to that. And I don't know, either, whether germs from dying sea birds can be transmitted to humans. If it is a form of pneumonia, the only one I know that does transfer between birds and man is psittacosis, bird-fancier's lung, and that's a chronic chest disease, like chronic bronchitis. To be frank, I don't think you should be handling the birds. I couldn't tell you for sure whether there's a risk or not, and it would be better to be safe than sorry.'

'I'll do what you say, Doc,' Charlie said, lifting the bird and wrapping it up again in the paper. Then he added, 'I've seen botulism before and it isn't like this. The birds stagger around, semi-paralysed, then lie on their backs and wave their legs and wings about weakly, till they die. It doesn't take long and they don't cough or produce this amount of mucus around their beaks. In any case only gulls scavenge – shags and cormorants eat only fresh fish, so they aren't exposed to botulism. My hunch, like yours, is that it's some form of infection, but it must be pretty powerful to hit so many birds of so many species, all at once. Could it be pollution – say, a poison in the sea, a discharge from shipping?'

'The only kind of discharge like that would be oil, wouldn't it?' I said. 'And there's no spill, is there, on the beach?'

Charlie shook his head.

'There's just one thing nagging at me,' he said. 'I've seen this once before, around ten years ago. Thousands of dead birds, around Christmas time. We never found the cause then. It took years before the populations of the different birds climbed back to normal. When I go home I'll look up my records to see when it was and I'll let you know.'

He turned to leave.

'Oh, and by the way, Merry Christmas,' he said. 'I hope you aren't too busy.'

Charlie left and I walked from the surgery through the short corridor to the main part of the house, sat down to have a coffee and to open the presents with Catriona, now a very active toddler, and Alasdair, who at fourteen months had just started to walk. Mairi was speaking on the phone.

'You have a call,' she said, once off the phone. 'It's at a place called Auchencleoch. It's one of the forestry houses on the hill road from Braehill to Glencree. Two youngsters have really bad coughs and are finding it difficult to breathe.'

'Youngsters? How old?' I asked her.

'Early teens,' she said. 'Their names are John and James Duggan: their father called. He is Daniel, his wife is Agnes, but I can't find them in the records. They must be new. He thinks the boys need urgent treatment. They haven't been ill like this before.'

I looked at the Ordnance Survey map for the district. The Braehill to Glencree road snaked up into the hills along the river valley for twenty miles. It took me a while to pinpoint Auchencleoch, hidden in the narrow contours a good three miles off the road, with a single dotted line winding up to it.

I screwed up my face. Single dotted lines meant an unmetalled single-track road, probably with gates and cattle grids, and usually plenty of potholes. I had never been called to the house before, and hadn't even known that people lived there, so far out of the way. I left Mairi and her mum, Bessie, to prepare the Christmas dinner, and walked out to the car.

It was one of those cold, frosty days with no cloud in the sky. The sun shone, but there was no heat in it. It took me twenty minutes to reach the makeshift sign on the Braehill to Glencree road that pointed the way to Auchencleoch. I blessed the weather. I had been right about the dotted line. The single-track road would have been a quagmire if its surface hadn't been solidified by the frost. I had to slow to around five miles an hour and sometimes slower to navigate the ruts, the holes and the rocks. Twice I had to get out to open and shut gates, put there to keep sheep in and deer out of the grazed moorland. About a mile along the road the forest started and the track improved a little. Auchencleoch was two miles into the forest.

The house, small and four-roomed, with smoke rising from the two chimneys, one at each gable end, had seen better days. The white paint was peeling, revealing patches of the grey stone underneath. Littered around the sides were rusting relics of farming and forestry machinery, and an old car that hens were using as a roost. There was no attempt to make a garden, though there was a square of ground a few yards away with some sad leeks and Brussels sprouts poking up from the frosted soil. Beside it a washing line held an assortment of clothes, white and stiff as boards. In a small paddock was a dejected donkey, and beyond was a pond, on which were some birds, possibly geese, maybe swans. They were just too far away to be seen clearly.

I walked to the door. Before I could knock, a man in his fifties greeted me and led me into the main room. He was big and burly, in a shirt opened at the neck, a waistcoat and old, baggy, thick tweed trousers. He hadn't shaved for days and looked tired and drawn.

A woman, thin and careworn, was sitting by the fire. She was about the same age as the man. I assumed she was Agnes. She smiled at me, but didn't rise or introduce herself.

'Dan Dougan,' the man said. 'Thanks for coming. I'd like you to see the boys. They have got really bad colds and can't shake them off.'

Bad colds, I thought, and he wants me to come all this way, on Christmas Day, just for that? But I was polite, smiled back at him, and let him lead me to the boys' room. They were lying side by side in single beds. They were flushed, finding it difficult to breathe, constantly coughing and holding their heads as they coughed. They told me that they had felt 'awful' for several days, had had shivers and sweats, had pains in their limbs and back, headaches, and couldn't breathe easily without their ribs hurting.

I listened to their chests, took their temperatures and pulse rates, and knew I wasn't dealing with colds. They had true influenza. I was curious about this, because they were the first cases in the district. In fact I didn't know of any cases in Scotland. There was nothing about an impending epidemic in the medical news or on the medical gossip grapevine.

Stranger still, the boys hadn't been anywhere to catch the 'flu. They had not been at school recently, they said, and in any case it was now the school holidays. They had been in and around the house for the last month and had met no one. The furthest they had been was to the pond to try to bag a bird.

'And did you bag one?' I asked.

'No,' the older one, John, said. 'There were a few dead ones lying around, so we thought they might be poisoned. So we left the rest alone.'

'Why would they be poisoned?' I asked. 'Who would do that?'

'The local gamekeepers leave poison around for the

buzzards, and we thought it might have got into the water,' said James. 'So we kept clear of them after that.'

'Did you touch any of the dead birds?'

'We buried four of them, just in case any animals might eat them and get sick themselves. So we touched them. But we washed afterwards.'

Curiouser and curiouser, I thought, then turned to their father.

'They both have chest infections, probably 'flu,' I told him. 'I'll give them antibiotics for now, and you can come to the surgery after Boxing Day for some more. Keep them in bed for the next two days and give them plenty of food and drinks. They'll take a while to recover completely, but they should be fine.'

He thanked me, I said goodbye to the boys, and we walked back into the main room.

A much younger woman had joined Agnes by the fireside, sitting beside her in an easy chair, her arms across a very large abdomen. I walked over to her and smiled.

'When's the baby due?' I asked.

'It's not very long now,' said Agnes. 'A few days, I suppose.'

'So, are you visiting?' I asked.

The younger woman looked puzzled.

'Why do you think that? I live here,' she replied.

'Then why haven't you been to see me?' I asked. 'Have you at least seen the nurse?'

'Oh, no,' said the older woman. 'We like to do this our way – we don't like clinics or hospitals for a natural thing like having children.'

'Natural isn't always the best,' I said. Turning to the young woman, I asked if she minded if I examined her. She didn't. In fact, she looked relieved.

I was shocked to find that she was in early labour and had a blood pressure that was going through the roof. If I didn't get her into the maternity unit in Girvan fast, we might have a tragedy on our hands. Her blood pressure rise meant that she was at extreme risk of having convulsions if we couldn't bring it down, and we plainly couldn't do that in Auchencleoch.

First, however, I had to know who she was. She didn't appear on my list of people signed to the practice. Dan explained that she was his stepdaughter Carol, the daughter of Agnes by a previous marriage. I didn't ask about the father-to-be, sensing that the answer might be difficult. Nor did I waste time probing why she had had no antenatal care.

I explained to them why she needed to be in hospital and used their phone to dial the ambulance service. The only available ambulance would take forty minutes to get to the house, so I decided to bundle her and Agnes in my car and meet the ambulance on the way. We left Dan to look after the boys.

Being rumbled about on a forestry road when in labour doesn't calm things down. Halfway to Girvan I had to stop to tend to Carol, who was now ready to push. As luck would have it, we were outside the only inn on the road. It would be easier to deliver the baby in a bed than in the car, so I sent Agnes off to the front door for help. She came back within seconds.

'The hotel is closed for Christmas,' she said, beginning to panic. 'There's no one here to give us a room.'

Just at that moment the ambulance drove up. The two ambulance men and I lifted Carol out of the car, placed her on a stretcher, and wheeled it into the back of the ambulance. That's where we delivered her of a healthy baby boy, seconds later.

I eventually sat down to my Christmas dinner a few hours late. It was worth waiting for. Sitting in the lounge with Mairi and Bessie afterwards, I mentioned that I had thought I was going to miss out on Christmas completely, and Bessie reminded me that I had had a more complete Christmas than most. After all, I had met a Christmas Carol and delivered her of a baby boy when there was no room at the inn.

Two days later, Carol and her new baby left the hospital against our advice. When I went back to Auchencleoch a day later to check up on her, the family had gone, taking with them their few sticks of furniture. They had left only the donkey, which the local innkeeper, now returned from Christmas, was glad to look after. We never heard where they went, or how they managed to survive. It turned out that they had been squatting in the house. The boys hadn't, in fact, been enrolled in the local school. We presumed that they didn't want to be traced officially for whatever reason, and it seemed unlikely that they had given me their real names.

The next day, the 'flu hit the practice with a vengeance. I had six calls that morning. The numbers expanded to twelve, then twenty and by the end of the week I was seeing thirty ill patients a day, and dealing with another twenty or more on the phone. Jimmy Anderson helped out, as did the two nurses, who both caught it and tried to struggle on.

Despite being in the midst of all these 'flu cases, I didn't catch it.

Charlie Welsh didn't catch it either. He came to see me on New Year's Eve.

'Remember I said that we've had a winter of bird

deaths before? It was 1957,' he said. 'The birds aren't dying any more,' he added. 'Whatever killed them seems to have passed. Do you know, it's a funny thing, but '57 was the only time I've had 'flu. Do you think there is a connection? I hear there's a lot of it about now.'

I remembered Christmas 1957, my first year at medical school, very clearly. I was in the university sanatorium – with 'flu. I still have the scar on my right lung to prove it. That winter hundreds of thousands of people all over Britain had caught the worst 'flu for many years.

'I've never heard of 'flu being transferred from birds to humans,' I said, 'but I suppose it's possible.'

I should have taken Charlie's suggestion more seriously. Nearly forty years later, the experts are worrying about people dying from bird 'flu in China, and they have uncovered a lot about how 'flu epidemics have spread via seabirds. They are fairly sure, for example, that the great pandemic (the Spanish 'flu) of 1918, which killed twenty million people in four months as it spread around the world, started with pigs. They are still puzzling over the epidemics of 1957, the Asian 'flu I caught as a student, and 1968, the Hong Kong 'flu that hit us that Christmas. They do know that people who caught the Asian 'flu were immune, as Charlie and I were, to the Hong Kong variety. The names relate to the first place that the 'flu virus was found. The puzzle for the British experts is that in 1957 the first case of Asian 'flu in Britain was reported from Stornoway, in the Outer Hebrides. In 1968 the Hong Kong 'flu started in the Black Isle, north of Inverness.

Why is that a puzzle? Because the 'flu virus, once you inhale it from another infected person, takes only two or three days to produce the illness. It doesn't make sense that the first cases would be in places so far from the usual ports of entry into Britain. Anyone carrying 'flu caught abroad would have become ill before they reached areas like Stornoway and the Black Isle. Far more feasible is a spread from the sea. Were those dead birds the real clue to the 'flu epidemics of 1957 and 1968? Charlie Welsh and I believe they were, but then, we're not experts.

Chapter Eighteen
Teeth...

Teeth have never been a favourite of mine. If I had wanted to deal with teeth, I would have been a dentist. That certainly was never my ambition. Don't get me wrong. I have good friends who are dentists. In fact I still run half marathons alongside my dentist, although he swears it's only so that I can see him in pain for a change.

My first school was in Glasgow – before my father's translation to Lincoln. I still remember my class teacher in that last year. Mrs Routledge (with the obvious nickname Rusty Legs) was large and fat, wore tweed suits, a stained cream blouse, thick stockings and brown brogues. I spent a lot of time looking down at those shoes, because it was her rule that we bowed our heads when she belted us.

It was Mrs Rusty Legs's wont to spend a substantial part of each day hitting her class of seven-year-olds with a belt – a mode of teaching that has thankfully fallen out of fashion. The official name for her instrument of torture was the Lochgelly tawse. A thick black leather strap with a divided end, like a snake's tongue, it was brought down on your hand with great force. It hurt badly enough when it hit the palms of your hands, but if her aim was out and it caught you across the wrist, that was really sore. Still, you stood and bore it, for even at seven years old you knew not to cry out. If you did you got another stroke. We all soon learned, too, that on the days her breath smelled stale and sweet, she was more likely to belt us and to hit our wrists, than on the days when it didn't.

We were belted if we were late for school in the morning, belted for talking in class, belted for not paying attention, belted for not being quick enough with our answers, indeed belted for anything Mrs Rusty Legs could find wrong that allowed her to inflict pain on us. I used to travel to school on the tramcar, and if the tram broke down and I had to run the last few hundred yards, rushing in at the last minute, breathless, I was belted.

Even if I had made the class in time, I was belted because I was out of breath.

What I remember most about Mrs Routledge were her teeth. They were long, yellow and crooked, splaying outwards, with the top ones overlapping the bottom lip so that she always looked as if she was biting it. Sometimes her gums showed, red and swollen. This arrangement of gums and protruding teeth gave her a permanent grimace that turned into a wide grin when she was angry with us.

Having teeth like that in those days was unusual. In the first half of the twentieth century it was common for people to have all their teeth pulled out, even if they were healthy, to prevent them from catching lethal infections like pneumonia or scarlet fever. It was thought that germs could get into your bloodstream through your teeth and gums, so in those days before penicillin, taking out all your teeth seemed a reasonable thing to do. That is why very few people had anything other than two perfect rows of shining white, even teeth, at least in public. In private, these 'perfect teeth' came out at every opportunity, even, or perhaps especially, at mealtimes. It was easier to chew with your gums than with the ill-fitting teeth that were issued by the average dentist. I remember my parents' bedroom, with 'his and hers' glasses by their bedside into which the teeth went every night. They told me about having their own teeth taken out at home, the job being done by a house-visiting dentist who used an ether rag and bottle, then took the teeth out in a great hurry before they 'came round'. The pain and nausea afterwards was almost unbearable.

So old Mrs Rusty Legs's teeth were most uncommon. We kids wondered, when we were able to talk in the playground, how they came to be so bad. We reckoned that she was scared of going to the dentist – she could dish pain out, but couldn't take it – a thought which gave us huge comfort.

Then one day she entered the class, tears running down her cheeks. She faced us, then said, 'Children, this is the saddest day in our history.'

The front wall of the room, behind her desk, was almost entirely filled by a blackboard fixed to the wall. Rolled up above the board was a huge map of the world. She tugged the cord at the side and the map unfurled. She called us to attention in our seats, then used her long wooden pointer to fix our eyes on the large red inverted triangle of British India.

'Today, India has betrayed our glorious Empire,' she said, sobbing. 'From now on, we will have to colour India green. The Union Flag will no longer fly over

India, and it will only be a matter of time before the rest of the red countries on this map will follow suit. You will live to see the end of the British Empire. I am glad that I will not.' She took out her handkerchief and blew her nose hard into it.

The boy sitting beside me dug me in the ribs and sniggered secretly at me, hugely amused by seeing our tormentor so upset. I grinned back at him and she saw me. I was called to the front. I had caught her on a bad day. Her breath was sickeningly sweet and sour at the same time. She gave me four strokes, two on one hand, two on the other. As I went back to my desk, I had my first political thought. If losing India had upset old Rusty Legs so much, it must be a very good thing.

One morning, about a month later, we had a new teacher. She was younger and kinder and liked to laugh a lot. Mrs Routledge never returned. We heard that she had become very ill and could no longer teach us. Only a short time afterwards she died. Years later, at medical school, I smelled breath like hers again. It was the odour of acetone. For the first time I felt sympathy for our persecutor. She had suffered badly from diabetes: it was probably the cause of her bad teeth and the reason why her dentist would have shied away from extracting them. At a stretch it might even have explained her bad moods and aggressive behaviour, although I don't think my forgiveness can stretch that far.

About two years into my time in Collintrae, our postman, Jackie Logan, knocked at the front door. He didn't usually knock: he just dropped my pile of journals, health service mail, drug company advertising and bills on the mat behind the open door and left, glad to offload his biggest burden of the day. This day, however, he wanted to see me.

'Morning, Doc,' he said. 'I wonder if you would call in on Miss Wallace at Tam's Well Cottage. When I left her mail today she wasn't looking so good and she didn't give me her usual banter. I don't know if she's ill, but I thought I'd better tell you.'

'I don't think I know her,' I said. 'She hasn't been to see me. Have you ever found her like this before?'

'No,' Jackie replied. 'She keeps herself to herself and doesn't get out much. All her groceries are delivered, and she has given up her car. And most of her friends are gone now.'

I told Jackie I'd see her, and walked into the surgery to look for her notes.

They were blank. Not just blank since I arrived, but blank since the official records were compiled at the beginning of the Health Service in 1948. There were no notes of any illnesses before that, either. It was usual for any pre-NHS notes to be stuffed into the cover of the NHS ones. Her notes were the thinnest of any I had met with in the practice – just an envelope with her name and date of birth and no contents.

I had a second 'take' at her date of birth. It showed her to be ninety-eight years old – and she was living by herself in a cottage three miles out of the village, with no other homes around her. A ninety-eight-year-old on her own with no neighbours usually meant a lot of work for doctor and nurse, but there was no evidence that she had bothered either.

The surgery finished early that morning, so I drove to Tam's Well wondering what she would be like. I walked up the winding path past flowering rose bushes and a manicured lawn to the front door. I could see, through the window, an elderly woman sitting hunched in a chair beside a fire. She was side-on to me, so that she didn't notice me until I rang the bell. Miss Wallace took a little time to rise and walk slowly to the door. It opened a little and she peered out.

'Wha're you?' she asked. 'Whit are ye daein' at ma door?'

There's nothing like politeness, I thought, and this was nothing like politeness.

'I'm the doctor. Jackie the Post asked me to call. He didn't think you were looking too well.'

She hesitated for a moment, then looked down at the bag in my hand and the stethoscope earpieces sticking out of my pocket. I must have convinced her I was the genuine article, because she stepped back, opened the door further and let me in.

'Jackie's got nae business callin' ye out on ma behalf, but seein' ye're here ye may as well hae a look at me,' she said. 'I dae hae a sair thrapple.'

So she had a sore throat, she looked flushed and she was cross. I wondered if she was always cross, or if illness had made her this way.

She settled in her chair and I asked her to open her mouth. She had two rows of perfect white teeth, even and strong – obviously false.

I smiled at her and asked the question that made me a laughing stock for years around the village.

'Could you take them out, please, so I can have a clearer view of your throat?'

'Tak' whit oot?' she said, indignant.

'Your teeth,' I replied. 'It's easier if the top plate doesn't fall down while I'm examining you.'

'Ah canna tak' them oot,' she almost shouted. 'They're a' ma ain.'

They were all her own. Miss Wallace, at ninety-eight, had thirty-two perfect teeth in her head. No fillings, no chips, no decay, and gums without a trace of swelling or recession. She was a miracle. Not only had she never seen a doctor, she hadn't seen a dentist, either.

I was no miracle, on the other hand. I wished the floor would open up and swallow me.

'Whit kind o' a doctor are you,' she continued, 'that canna tell real teeth frae wallies?'

Then, thankfully, she laughed. 'Wait till ah tell my freens aboot this yin,' she said.

Things proceeded a little better after that. Her throat was sore, and I started her on her first-ever course of penicillin. She asked me to have a cup of tea with her and then sprung her next surprise. She went to the door of the room and called up the stairway.

'Effie, will ye come doon a minute? I'd like the doctor tae see ye.'

I heard a door close and footsteps come to the top of the stairs. I joined Miss Wallace at the foot of the stairs and, looking up, saw Effie. She was small, thin and stooped, with balding grey hair. She wore a long, grey woollen skirt and a blouse and cardigan that had seen better days, but were clean and tidy. She walked down the stairs very carefully and slowly. She looked dully at me, then at Miss Wallace, who smiled at her. She didn't smile back, but shuffled past us into the sitting room and sat down in a chair in the corner.

'Effie's been a bit off-colour for a day or two. I wondered if she has the same throat as me. Could ye tak a look at it?' Miss Wallace asked.

'Sure,' I said. 'Hello, Effie,' I said. I offered her my hand to shake. 'I'm the doctor. Are you not feeling well?' Effie looked at my hand, a frown on her face, glanced at Miss Wallace, then stared back at me. She kept her hands on her lap and didn't reply.

Miss Wallace smiled at me and shrugged. 'Effie won't answer you,' she said. 'She doesn't speak. But I know how she is when she's feeling no' weel, and this is one o' thae times. She'll let you look at her. It's just that she isn't used tae men aboot the hoose.'

I turned back to Effie and gave her my best reassuring smile. 'Could I look at your throat?' I asked. She glanced again at Miss Wallace, who nodded, and she opened her mouth. She too had two rows of fine white filling-free teeth.

I looked back at Miss Wallace and grinned.

'Dinna ask,' she said, laughing. 'They're her ain, too.'

Effie had the same sore throat. I rummaged in my bag for another bottle of penicillin tablets.

'She's not allergic to antibiotics?' I asked.

'She's never had them,' was the reply.

'Then it's safe to give them,' I said and handed over the pills. Miss Wallace took them and told Effie kindly that she could go back upstairs to her room. Effie stood up and walked out without saying a word. I watched her struggling up the stairs and heard the door shut above us.

I still didn't know who she was, but I knew what was wrong. Not from my medical training, but from my days as a nurse in the Lincoln hospital. The lack of emotion, the inability or unwillingness to talk, the blind acceptance of what was happening to her – all suggested a long-standing mental illness or handicap. But who was she?

Miss Wallace explained. More than fifty years before, she had signed up with the local mental health authorities to take in 'boarded-out patients'. The system was unique to Scotland. People who could not cope independently in normal society, but who were no risk to others or to themselves, were offered as permanent 'guests' to families who would give them a home and company. The council found maintaining the boarded-out system much cheaper than keeping people in hospital, so they paid the costs. Miss Wallace had received a small cheque each week for over half a century: it kept her and Effie comfortable and they didn't need much. Everything they ate came from their vegetable garden, their hens, their sheep and their cow. They made their own bread, and their own clothes from the wool. They were true crofters, working their two acres of ground behind the cottage together.

Effie's real name was Euphemia Morrison. She was twenty-seven when she was 'given' to Miss Wallace: she was now eighty-one. The two women had lived together in harmony all those years without bothering anyone. They didn't really want to bother me. Nor did they wish to bother the authorities. Miss Wallace was worried that someone at 'the office' might realise how old she was and take Effie away from her. Without Effie, she said, she would have little to live for, and Effie was a great help around the house and garden. The boarded-out scheme had stopped years ago – the two of them had somehow been forgotten and left alone. The money kept coming in from a trust fund set up before the war by the local authority of the time, and while Effie was alive, it would keep coming. Miss Wallace pleaded with me to let things continue as they were, and I was happy to agree.

As for the teeth, Miss Wallace put their health down to their water supply, which came from a spring in the hillside above the cottage. I didn't express an opinion. Back at the surgery I found the notes of Miss Euphemia Morrison. They were almost as thin as Miss Wallace's. Except that they contained a letter dated 1912, from a hospital doctor to the GP in Collintrae at the time.

It explained that Miss Morrison had been mute since the age of fifteen, when she had been found alone in her home beside her dead mother. How her mother had died was unclear. There were suspicions that Euphemia had had something to do with the death, but it could not be proved. She was obviously ill, with what was labelled then as 'dementia praecox', and would now be called paranoid schizophrenia. After twelve years in hospital, it had been decided that she was harmless and could be boarded out. Miss Wallace's home had been inspected and found to be ideal. The only other notes in Euphemia's record were acknowledgments of annual visits made by the mental health authorities until 1945. After that, nothing. It seemed that there was no one left who knew about them.

I read the letter again and remembered Mr Evans and Mr Brown from my time in Lincoln. I wondered how safe Miss Wallace really was, then dismissed the thought. Should I explain my worries to the current psychiatric team? If I did, they would take Effie away, and that would

be the end of Miss Wallace. If I didn't, they would probably continue to live amicably together. I decided to say
nothing.

Miss Wallace survived until she was one hundred and
seven, sharp as a needle to the end. Euphemia died aged
eighty-eight, two years before her, peacefully in her bed,
never having spoken a word until her last few moments.
All she said then, quietly, to Miss Wallace was 'Thank
you'.

Chapter Twenty
Goodbyes

Jenny looked up at me and smiled. 'You know, Doctor,' she whispered, 'my mother wanted to call me Victoria. But my dad didn't like the name. It would have been funny, wouldn't it, if he had?' Almost imperceptibly, her head shifted back into the pillow. The smile stayed for a while, then slowly faded. Her eyes didn't close: they kept staring, steadily, into mine. But they were not seeing me. Mrs Jenny Plum had kept up her good humour to the end.

It was three in the morning. The light beside her hospital bed in the small side-ward was dimmed, the hospital eerily silent, as if all the rest of life had stopped just for this moment. I gently stretched my hand out to close her eyes, and tiptoed out through the gap between the curtains to tell the night sister.

That was more than forty years ago. I've never forgotten Jenny. We had met at the hospital outpatient clinic only a month before. Just twenty-three, she was thrilled to be pregnant. Everything was fine, except that her abdomen was much bigger than it should have been for its 'dates'. She had joked about that, too.

'If I keep on like this,' she had laughed, 'I'll have quins – or an elephant.' I didn't laugh with her. I had only read about this type of pregnancy in the textbooks. Inexperienced as I was, I feared the worst. I knew it could be a chorionepithelioma, a form of cancer of the placenta that was fatal within a few weeks. I called the consultant, who felt her abdomen, nodded briefly to me, and calmly arranged admission to the ward.

We didn't tell patients the truth in those days. The chief decided that we were to call the problem a 'malformation' that would need time to cure, and that it would be best for her to stay in hospital in the meantime. He also decreed that we should keep her and her husband in the dark until the last possible moment. He then left the details of her care to the nurses and to me, the most junior doctor.

I realise now that she knew the truth from the start.

307

She just didn't want me to know that she knew, so she played along with the charade. I learned so much from her about how to die with courage and dignity, and all I could offer her in return was my company as often as I could spare it. Her husband visited less and less, and once he was told that there was no hope, he stopped coming, because he couldn't lie to her face. He was only twenty-two himself, and I'm sure Jenny understood why he couldn't face her, and forgave him for his absence in her final week.

By the end of my fourth year in Collintrae, I was facing a similar problem, but it was much more personal. Bessie, Mairi's mother, had fought breast cancer for nearly ten years, and was now living out her last few months in our home. Like Jenny, she never complained, and also like Jenny, she knew that her case was hopeless. Yet she didn't talk about it to Mairi or myself until her last evening.

It was Prince Charles's twenty-first birthday, and there was a television programme about him and the Royal Family that she wanted to watch. As it ended, she turned to us and said 'I'm finished.'

I helped her upstairs to her bedroom, and Mairi put her to bed. Catriona, now aged four, padded through in her slippers to kiss Grandma goodnight. Alasdair remained in his cot, sound asleep. Bessie, lying back against the pillows, looked at me and asked for her injection: she was on a cocktail of drugs to ease her pain, now constant. Jenny came into my mind as I slid the needle under her skin. As I removed it, Bessie turned her head slightly and gave a sigh. She smiled wanly at her granddaughter, then fell asleep.

She didn't wake up. The next morning we had a lot of thinking to do. The practice had grown in numbers and in workload over the four years. Surgeries were busier, there were more calls for visits, and medicine had changed. We had far better drugs to treat asthma, high blood pressure, heart disease, infections, stomach ulcers and diabetes, but they came with a high price, not in money, but in the need to follow up patients with all these illnesses. It meant establishing regular clinics for them all, employing staff, enlarging premises and constantly keeping up to date with all the medical innovations.

It was obvious that the practice needed another doctor. It was also obvious that Mairi needed help. She was the receptionist, practice manager, dispenser and patient pacifier when I wasn't immediately available. She was on call day and night just as much as I was. Except that she wasn't paid for her work. At that time doctors' wives could not be paid: they were expected to give their services to the practice free.

It was clear that if the local medical committee did not provide the funds for a second doctor, we would have to rethink our future. Now that Bessie was gone, we had no family commitment to the area. If we had to leave I would deeply regret leaving the patients, but the rest of the family needed a break. Mairi required a lot more support than I could offer with my limited time in the home, and the children needed to see me as a father, not as a stranger who was only home when they rose in the morning and after they had been put to bed at night. I wrote to the local health authority about the possibility of creating another GP position in the district. The reply was curt and to the point. Of course I could have a partner, provided his or her salary came out of my pocket. So we started to look around for a new life.

What could we do? I wasn't keen to go back into partnership: my Birmingham experience had soured me for that. It would be good to do something different for a while, perhaps a nine-to-five job that would give us some family life. But what? Medicine didn't offer many jobs like that.

The first three months of any year are hard for single-handed country doctors, with their toll of illness and extra deaths among the elderly. They are not so bad if there are plenty of days of sunshine and calm weather, but during bouts of wet and cold people fall prey easily to depression and feeling unwell. Surgery attendances rise and the numbers of home calls rocket.

As if to test my already waning endurance, from January to April 1970 we had relentless rain and wind. Storm after storm hit the Ayrshire coast, the toll on the people of the Stinchar Valley was heavy, and the workload for the practice, and for Mairi especially, was exhausting. We knew by Easter that we had to get out. My journal reading started with the 'Appointments Vacant' column rather than the editorials.

In early May, one of these appointments caught my eye. It was for a doctor to join the research team of a drugs company. It would mean learning about the development of new treatments and organising their trials in university departments all over Britain. That sounded interesting, but what really struck me was the name at the bottom of the advertisement. Vivian Lewis had been one of my tutors at Birmingham: I reasoned that if he was heading the group I would get a good training and would have an extra string to my medical bow. On impulse, I phoned him. He remembered me, and instead of asking me to come for an interview, said that he would travel up to Collintrae in a week's time, to interview me at home.

The day of the interview started badly and got worse. The telephone wakened me at seven in the morning. It was Duggie Shearer, whose farm, Ailsa Mains, ran along the coast north of Collintrae. He sounded in a panic.

'Doc, could you come at once?' he said. 'I've got six men here who've had heart attacks in the night. They're a' writhin' aboot in agony wi' chest pain.'

One heart attack in a night for any doctor is commonplace. Two is stretching it a bit. Three is unheard of. But six!

'Hold on,' I said, 'I'm coming, but first I need to know a bit about them. Who are they and when did their pains start?'

'They're howkers,' he said. 'This morning, when they woke up, they could hardly breathe, the pains in their chests were so bad. They cannae get up from their mattresses. They're yellin' and screamin' wi the pain. Ye'll need tae dae something.'

Howkers were a very special group of people. They came to Ayrshire every year from May onwards, to pick, or 'howk' potatoes. The 'Tattie Master', Hugh Gibson, lived in Fife. The farmers planted the tatties in January, and Gibson organised the harvest four months later.

Once the crop was ready for lifting, he brought over, by lorry, hundreds of 'howkers' from Ireland, from County Cavan and County Clare. They lived in sheds and byres provided by the farmer, and by day followed the machines that turned over the ground and spewed the potatoes over the earth. It was back-breaking work that lasted from dawn to dusk, bending, lifting, heaving, sorting and bagging the potatoes. The howkers were exhausted by the end of the day, going back to their sheds only to eat and to sleep. They were so tired that nothing would waken them in the night. They slept the sleep of the dead each night, in rows, on mattresses and on the straw, usually fully dressed, ready just to wash in the yards and be transported to the fields each morning. I would see them occasionally at the surgery for minor injuries. They were great people, hard-working and never complaining, however rough their lot was. They sent most of their pay home, only holding a little back for a few essentials each week.

When I arrived, I could see I had a real emergency on my hands. The patients were lying, some on their backs, some on their sides, moaning and clutching their chests. They were all in one area, partitioned off from the rest of the men and women by a wooden wall. The rest of their group were standing around, anxious and completely at a loss at what to do. They parted to let me through to the scene of the 'epidemic'.

There were, in fact, seven men lying in the section. The six nearest me were the ones with the sore chests. The seventh was lying in the corner, curled up in a ball, sound asleep, facing the wall. I bent down to talk to the first man. He was holding his arms across his chest, hugging himself tightly. He explained that it was the only way he could breathe without great pain. I could see that he was breathing only with his diaphragm – his stomach was rising and falling with each breath, but he was making sure that his ribs weren't moving. I looked briefly across at the others. They were all doing the same: whether they were on their sides or on their backs, they were desperate not to move their chest muscles.

'When did this start?' I asked the man nearest me.

'I woke up with it,' he said, grimacing at the effort he had to make just to speak. 'So did all the others.'

The second and third men nodded their agreement. It seemed that they had all wakened early, around five in the morning, with pains in their chests. Only when the gaffer had come round to wake them up at seven were they able to tell him about their strange affliction.

I had not the slightest idea what this could be or why,

for that matter, the man in the corner could have slept through it all. I asked the first man to open his shirt, so that I could examine him more closely. It took a major effort from him to lever himself up into a half-seated position, unbutton his shirt and lift up his vest.

The front of his chest showed a series of disc-shaped red spots about a centimetre across, two or three centimetres apart. When I put pressure on his chest he yelped. Pressure from the sides hurt a lot, too. He had severely bruised, if not broken ribs. The chests of all the other men in pain showed exactly the same marks and they had the same signs of rib damage.

The cause was beginning to dawn on me. I asked the first man when they had gone to bed.

'We all went to sleep about midnight,' he said, 'except for Sean over there in the corner.'

Sean was snoring peacefully, still curled against the wall.

'So when did he get to bed?' I asked.

'We don't know,' said the man. 'He was out on the batter, and we must have been asleep when he came in.'

'But he would have had to climb over you to get to his place, wouldn't he?' I asked.

'To be sure,' he replied.

I stepped gingerly between the men over to Sean in

the corner. He smelled very strongly of whisky, was unconscious to the world, and on his feet were his hobnailed boots – in the vernacular, 'tackety bits'. The hobnails matched exactly the pattern of spots on each man's chest. Sean's boots were the cause of all their concerns.

I could do little to help them all, other than to prescribe some painkillers and suggest that they get up and about as soon as they could bear the pain. They were a gentle lot, so they forgave Sean his walk over them, but I heard later that he was condemned after that to the spot nearest the door, where the wind and the rain would punish him for his transgression.

I drove back home and prepared myself for the morning surgery and for the interview that was scheduled for around noon. The surgery passed routinely until the phone rang again. This time it was Willie Tait, the polis.

'Sorry about this, Doc,' he said, 'but we need you straight away, at Cranhill. We've got a man on the roof and he's slinging slates at us. We gather he needs some counselling.'

Cranhill was an isolated house about six miles away, on a side road in the hills. It had a driveway about forty metres long sloping down to the front door. Built on the

'He smelled very strongly of whisky, was unconscious to
the world, and on his feet were his hobnailed boots – in
the vernacular, "tackety bits". The hobnails matched
exactly the pattern of spots on each man's chest.'

side of a hill, it had a sheer drop behind down to the River Tig, a tributary of the Stinchar, about a hundred feet below.

I knew who the man was without being told. David Marshbank had been a family doctor in Bristol for many years. Then, in his fifties, he had been sued by a patient's widow. It was something to do with a wrong diagnosis that had led to the patient's death, and the widow had blamed the doctor. I never knew the details, but sympathised with him. It happens at some time in our career to many of us, and we have to develop a thick skin to survive a case like this.

Dr Marshbank's skin was not thick enough. He had broken under the strain and had had to retire from practice. He felt that his fellow doctors had not given him enough support at the time and that he had been unjustly pursued in the courts and ignored by his local medical committee. He had had to leave his old practice area, and he and his wife had taken the Cranhill house as a hideaway from the realities of their lives.

It hadn't worked. Over the months that followed he had changed. He started speaking in French, a language that he had not used since his schooldays. He put up notices around the outside of the house, in his garden and at the gate, in French, for people to stay away or be *'fusillé'*. He would remonstrate in French against anyone walking by his door. Naturally, as most of them were locals, they hadn't understood a word. Everyone gave him a wide berth, which was sad, because he and his wife became ever more isolated and cut off from their new community.

I told Mairi where I was going and left the Cranhill number so that Dr Lewis could phone if he arrived before I returned. She wasn't happy that I was going to visit someone who was throwing slates about, but there was no alternative. It was all part of the job.

I arrived at the same time as the fire brigade, old friends from my trips down cliffs. The ambulance was already there, along with two police cars. Those who had been brave enough to get out of their vehicles were standing behind the thick trunk of a large old yew tree in the front garden. The side of the tree facing the house had six or seven slates embedded in it at around head height.

On the roof, busy prising yet another missile from it, was Dr Marshbank. He was amazingly nimble for his sixty years. He had seen my car pull up and stopped his fumbling with the slate.

'*Ah, le médecin est arrivé,*' he shouted. '*Va t'en, Docteur. Ce n'est pas ton affaire.*'

I went to stand behind the yew tree with the police inspector, and he filled me in on what had happened. A holidaymaker had passed by the house early that morning and had been told to go away or be shot. The visitor's response had been to call the police, who had duly arrived in a car with blue light flashing. That was mistake number one.

The second mistake was to try to arrest the doctor. He had run upstairs, climbed like a cat burglar out of the dormer window and walked up the slates onto the apex of the roof that stretched between the chimneys at the gable ends. There he would stay until all the 'foreigners' left his premises.

No one was going to leave him in that state, and when this dawned on him, he had started throwing slates. One or two had narrowly missed the police officers, and when Willie Tait arrived as support, he had suggested me as their saviour.

I wasn't feeling best pleased with Willie at this point, but had to concede that Dr Marshbank needed medical help. Somehow we had to persuade him down from the roof and get him to a place of safety – which for the time being meant the Ayr psychiatric unit.

The slates stopped flying, and Dr Marshbank took to walking along the rooftop between the two chimneys. It looked a dangerous pastime, as the top tiles were curved, and the balance needed for the feat was similar to that of a tightrope walker. He didn't seem in the least unsteady as he watched us, while keeping up his walk. He would turn at each chimney and walk back without a hint that he might fall.

'Someone had better go up there and try to talk to him,' I said. The police inspector, Willie, the fire chief and the ambulance man all agreed, then looked at me.

'I'm not good at heights,' I said, weakly.

'You're the professional, Doc,' said Willie, not unkindly.

The firemen pushed a ladder up against the wall. No slates came our way. Dr Marshbank looked on curiously from his perch, leaning against one chimney, saying nothing. The top of the ladder rested above the guttering, and a hefty fireman stayed at the bottom to hold it in place. I walked forward and started to climb. The slate-thrower stayed where he was, watching me closely. I clambered onto the roof.

The firemen then passed me up a shorter ladder with a hook at the end, to fix it over the top of the roof. I slid it upwards, and it held fast. Dr Marshbank allowed me to climb up it, laboriously, flattening myself against the rungs as I did so. I reached the top and sat astride the roof, facing him, at which point it started to rain. I felt the cold water permeate through my trousers. I shuffled towards him, inch by inch, unable to loosen my grip of the rooftop for fear of falling.

My quarry was now facing me, angry that I had invaded his space. He towered above me, drawing himself fully upright, standing on the top of the roof, not even holding onto the chimney with one hand.

He put his right hand into his jacket pocket and drew out a black object that I couldn't at first see in detail: my glasses were covered with raindrops and I had to take them off and wipe them with a handkerchief. I shuffled closer, saying to him that I just wanted to speak to him, and had no intention of harming him.

The lenses now clear, I saw that the object was a children's toy gun, just like the ones you could buy from Woolworths. He waved it at me, up and down.

'If you come any nearer, I'll shoot,' he shouted, this time in English. I was encouraged by the change of language. That seemed to suggest that he was perhaps a little closer to normality than a few minutes before. I shuffled forward again, near enough to reach his outstretched hand.

'Be careful,' I said. 'Waving that about might make you fall. I'll just take it.'

'I reached the top and sat astride the roof, facing him... he
towered above me, drawing himself fully upright, not even
holding onto the chimney with one hand... "If you come
any nearer I'll shoot," he shouted.'

I simply reached forward and pulled the toy gun from his hand. It was heavier than I thought it would be. I tossed it down to the ground beside the police inspector and edged a little closer. All I wanted to do was to talk for a while, to try to calm him.

I had obviously got too close. Two events followed in quick succession. First, Dr Marshbank made a run for it. He jumped down to the top of the dormer window, used the finial above it as a lever, and swung out into space. For a moment I thought he was lost – falling over the side of the roof onto the hillside far below us. But he was more agile than I thought. His body described a graceful arc in space and he crashed downwards feet first through the glass of the window into the bedroom below. I heard later that he had been 'apprehended' there by two burly ambulance men and quickly sedated with an injection.

Why did I hear this later? Because of the second event.

While I was beginning to back off the roof, still straddling it, towards the ladder, there was a loud bang from the garden below. I peered though my wet glasses to see the inspector gazing at the barrel of the toy gun. There was now a bullet hole in the yew tree alongside the slates.

The inspector looked up at me.

'That was a real gun, Doc. You were bloody lucky,' he called.

I'd like to say I took the news in my stride, but I didn't. I clung to the sides of the roof with all four limbs and started to shiver. I shook so hard that I dislodged even more slates. I couldn't stop shivering. I was totally unable to move my arms and legs.

One of the firemen leapt up the ladders to reach me and carried me down in a genuine fireman's lift. I was hardly able to stand when I reached the ground. The enormity of the risk I had taken had reduced me to a shaking wreck. I was helped to my car, and Willie Tait offered to drive me home. As I sat in the passenger seat, a man walked over to greet me.

It was Vivian Lewis. He had witnessed the whole event, from the moment I had climbed onto the roof.

'You have got the job,' he said, grinning. 'I'd better get you out of this practice before you get killed.'

***

We left Collintrae three months later, to start our new life. We didn't use the brick lorry for the move. The last few weeks were heartrending as we said goodbye to so many patients who had become friends, and to all our colleagues. Leaving the house was a wrench, too, but it was tempered by the fact that we had bought a cottage in the district, between Kilminnel and Braehill, where we would return as often as possible.

The new job was certainly different. In the beginning I saw much more of the children, and Mairi could devote her time to them as she had never been able to before. We found out what was causing Catriona's infections. A year after the move, she developed appendicitis, and at the operation the surgeon found that the appendix had been lying across her ureter – the tube between the right kidney and the bladder. The infections stopped when the offending appendix was removed. She never looked back.

Dr Marshbank responded excellently to treatment, becoming completely well and living another twenty years happily at Cranhill. He never spoke French again. One day he and his wife were picnicking on the Collintrae beach when two young boys got into trouble in the receding tide. He responded to their calls for help by running into the sea and rescuing them, pulling them safely to shore before collapsing and dying where he lay. He was in his eightieth year.

The tattie howkers were replaced by machinery in the late 1980s, and a lot of colour went out of the

Collintrae scene when they disappeared.

I was replaced by two doctors, a man and wife team who worked together for one salary. So the local medical committee had their wish of employing two doctors for the cost of one. Thankfully, that has changed. More than thirty years later, the practice has two-and-a-half doctors (one works part-time in the district general hospital). They are paid and supported appropriately. It's a good arrangement, they are excellent doctors and I count them as good friends.

After seven years in the south we returned to the Stinchar Valley to write and to help out friends as their locum. From time to time I still work in Collintrae for a day or so, which is how I know how my old patients and friends are managing. I do regular locum stints for other doctor friends along the Solway coast and occasionally in the Highlands and Islands. General practice is different now, and the old doctor-patient relationship has gone, replaced by a more efficient Health Service machine. We are told it's better for both patients and doctors, but I miss it.

Doctor, have you got a minute?
Dr Tom Smith answers all those health questions
you've never dared ask
1-904977-79-0 Paperback   £9.99

Tom Smith is the doctor you've always dreamed of…

You might make an appointment with your GP to enquire about a high fever or a septic toe. But when do you get to ask the questions you really want the answers to? All those health mysteries – the trivial, the serious, the downright weird – that you never get an opportunity to ask a doctor about …

How long can we live? Why do women start growing hair on their chins at 35? Why do we cry? Is a man's hand size really a sign of the length of his penis?

This is your chance to corner a doctor at a party and boldly go where no patient has gone before. Whether you're a beauty junky, a neurotic mum or a midlife male, Dr Tom Smith has the answers. Funny, unshockable, sharp as a scalpel, he will satisfy your concern and curiosity with a wit and wisdom that your own doctor just never seems to have time for.

How to Be a Bad Birdwatcher

To the greater glory of life

Simon Barnes

1-904977-05-7 Paperback   £7.99

Look out of the window.
See a bird.
Enjoy it.
Congratulations. You are now a bad birdwatcher.

Anyone who has ever gazed up at the sky or stared out of the window knows something about birds. In this funny, inspiring, eye-opening book, Simon Barnes paints a riveting picture of how birdwatching has framed his life and can help us all to a better understanding of our place on this planet.

How to be a Bad Birdwatcher shows why birdwatching is not the preserve of twitchers, but one of the simplest, cheapest and most rewarding pastimes around.

"A delightful ode to the wild world outside
the kitchen window"
Daily Telegraph

The Good Granny Guide
Or how to be a modern grandmother
Jane Fearnley-Whittingstall
1-9040977-70-7 Paperback £8.99

In *The Good Granny Guide*, Jane Fearnley-Whittingstall provides a wonderfully entertaining insight into the joys – and pitfalls – of being a grandmother. A closely involved granny of five, she has gathered first-hand tips from other grandparents and their families in many different situations. The result is a vast resource of practical ideas to help you make the most of the time you spend with your grandchildren, plus invaluable advice on everything from childcare troubleshooting to what NOT to say to the daughter-in-law.

"Sound on everything from nappies to tantrums.
Jane Fearnley-Whittingstall gets the golden
rules right. She is spot on"
Philip Howard, *The Times*

"Gives tips on how to spoil the grandkids
wihout ruining your relationship with
their Mum and Dad"
Woman's Own

Amo, amas, amat... and all that

How to become a Latin lover

Harry Mount

1-9040977-54-5 Hardback £12.99

Have you ever found yourself irritated when a *sine qua non* or a *mea culpa* is thrown into the conversation by a particularly annoying person? Or do distant memories of afternoons spent struggling to learn obscure verbs fill you with dread?

Never fear! (or as a Latin show-off might say, *Nil Desperandum!*) In this delightful guided tour of Latin, which features everything from a Monty Python grammar lesson to David Beckham's tattoos and all the best snippets of prose and poetry from 2000 years of literary history, Harry Mount wipes the dust off those boring primers and breathes life back into the greatest language of them all.

"Mount's love of Latin shines out on every page"
Spectator

"This breezy guide to the Latin language sugars the grammatical pill with well-placed jokes and friendly 'I'm on your side' advice"
Mary Beard, *Daily Telegraph*

The Meaning of Sport

Simon Barnes

1-9040977-45-6 Hardback £16.99

In *The Meaning of Sport*, award-winning sports writer Simon Barnes gives you his grandstand seat for a journey from the Olympic Games in Athens to the World Cup in Germany – via the Ashes series, the Ryder Cup, Wimbledon, and more. He examines why sport holds us all in such thrall, how it uplifts and crushes us – and can seem to matter more than life itself. He challenges us to recognise the intelligence of Wayne Rooney, the making of Freddie Flintoff, the mythic nature of Steve Redgrave; and he ponders the ultimate cruelty of the game.

This is the book which asks the questions no one else has thought of, and finds some surprising answers. Sport has never been written about like this before.

"His book is a delight: full of wisdom, humour and whimsy and shows that, when done well, sports books can compete on any level"
Michael Atherton